I *Refuse* to Lead a Dying Church!

I Refuse
TO LEAD A
DYING
CHURCH!

Paul Nixon

THE PILGRIM PRESS
CLEVELAND

Dedicated

*to the people who will
soon discover the joy of
exploring and celebrating
Christian faith in one of
our mainline churches*

The Pilgrim Press, 700 Prospect Avenue, Cleveland, Ohio 44115-1100
thepilgrimpress.com
© 2006 by Paul Nixon

Scripture quotations, unless otherwise noted, are from the New Revised
Standard Version of the Bible, © 1989 by the Division of Christian Education of
the National Council of Churches of Christ in the United States of America and
are used by permission. Changes have been made for inclusivity.

♲ Printed in the United States of America on acid-free paper that contains
30% post-consumer fiber.

12   11   10   09   08   10   9   8   7   6

Library of Congress Cataloging-in-Publication Data
Nixon, Paul, 1962–
    I refuse to lead a dying church! / Paul Nixon.
        p. cm.
    ISBN 978-0-8298-1759-1 (alk. paper)
    1. Church renewal.   I. Title.
BV600.3.N59 2006
262.001'7—dc22   2006037283

CONTENTS

ACKNOWLEDGMENTS

SPECIAL THANKS to judicatory leaders Paul Borden, Larry Goodpaster, and Paul Nickerson for their reflections on the manuscript and their lively conversation around the key themes, summarized in the epilogue! My gratitude also to Uli Guthrie, my editor at The Pilgrim Press, for her expertise and cheerful help in bringing this book to print.

INTRODUCTION

Is it possible to be a faithful servant of the Resurrected Christ and serve as pastor within one of the mainline denominations?

Most of the denominational faith communities that first evangelized North America are now rapidly down-shifting toward oblivion and near extinction. Most mainline pastors are leading churches that will not exist by the year 2100; many of these churches will be gone long before that. More than half of the congregations that call themselves United Methodist, Evangelical Lutheran, Presbyterian, Episcopal, Disciples of Christ, American Baptist, and United Church of Christ will likely disappear sometime in the next half-century. Thousands of future pastors currently training in university divinity schools will soon graduate full of zest for ministry, only to find themselves deployed to do deathbed vigil somewhere— tending a rapidly aging congregation that has little energy to do what's necessary to thrive.

In the largest of the old tribes, the United Methodist Church, the annual stockholders' report recently came down again, reporting a net membership loss for the thirty-seventh consecutive year. It's the same story in most groups; I simply highlight their story because they are the biggest ship sinking and it happens to be the one I'm on. During the past four decades of ecclesiastical and corporate rot, United Methodists lost half of their market share in the United States, as measured by members per capita. Other old denominations have suffered similar trends.[1]

If sociologist George Barna's predictions come true, the more evangelical denominations and regions may soon be joining their more liberal counterparts in this decline. Barna's observations go beyond mere acknowledgement of consumerism in American religion; his research is uncovering a generation of Americans no longer trusting any one religious institution or community to meet all their spiritual needs or to justify the full range of their spiritual commitments. He sees a rising nation of spiritual free agents, beholden to no church. Many of the nouveau unchurched continue to identify themselves as theists and Christians, and even to practice their faith with some intentionality.[2] A growing number of people will associate with organized churches only when those places "work for them" in their personal quests for meaningful theology, community, and service.

1. The Disciples of Christ lost 70 percent of market share in this same period, the United Church of Christ, 60 percent, and most of the major groups lost at least 40 percent. The Southern Baptists held their market share during this period, due in part to exuberant new church development; in fact, they claim to have increased it slightly. However, public polling does not corroborate Southern Baptist statistics, and they resist cleaning church rolls more than do other groups. See www.demographia.com/db-religlarge.htm and also the United Methodist History and Archives website.
2. George Barna, *Revolution* (Wheaton, Ill.: Tyndale House, 2005).

No persons or organizations want to believe they are really dying. It is natural for us to respond initially to a bad prognosis with denial, lifting up any statistic that helps us to maintain our denial. For example, up until recently, even as church membership numbers plummeted, United Methodist average *worship attendance* had only slipped by a net loss of 1 percent across these many years. This latter statistic provoked hope among some church leaders that what they were seeing was simply a downturn in "joining for joining's sake." But then came 2002 and 2003, and then 2004, when suddenly, after thirty-four years of an attendance plateau, the denominational Titanic lurched and keeled over. For the first time, worship attendance declined almost as fast as membership, not just for one year, but for three in a row. The United Methodists saw an unprecedented loss of 150,000 people in worship attendance over just three years.[3] (The United Methodists have sixty-five regions in the United States. Losing the equivalent of one whole region of worshippers every year now means that anyone under the age of forty reading this could potentially be the person who quietly turns out the lights and locks the last church door. What a cheery thought.)

For some of us enjoying our covered dish dinner on the gently sloping deck of our denominational ship, this downward attendance lurch caused our ice tea to tip over. The jazz ensemble slipped a note or two. Looks of concern darted from one eye to another. Then some of us suddenly realized: "This ship is *really* going down, all the way down, down to the bottom of the sea."

3. Based on national membership and attendance numbers for the United Methodist Church, 2002–2004, as supplied by the United Methodist Board of Global Ministries statistician, John Southwick.

So, given this grim state of affairs, I repeat the opening question: *Is it possible to be servants of a Resurrected Christ while serving as pastor to such a church?* I believe it is possible. But this is not a season for business as usual! In most of the old American denominations, there are two key realities: a sea of dying congregations and a much smaller network of creative, innovative community-minded churches that are thriving, almost oblivious to the trends in their larger denominational family. Though as a group these thriving churches are skewed to the right theologically, individually they range all over the map. They have some important things in common, as we will see in the pages ahead. Chief among them is the pastor's single-minded commitment to seeking out and fostering life.

I believe God invites every church to thrive. The fact that you're reading this book presumably means that you want to believe that too.

If the point were simply to encourage the development of theologically conservative churches and slowly, gently, lay the more liberal churches to rest, we would be walking away from faith engagement with a significant segment of American society—those persons who are more likely to explore Christian faith in a less dogmatic climate. Or if the point were simply to focus on the places where numerical growth is most likely, we could just walk away from most of our central city neighborhoods and do church on the edge of town where the subdivisions are still going in. These ideas are not the point, nor do I recommend them. Instead I believe that God invites every church in every sort of community setting to thrive!

SIX VITAL CHOICES

This short book is a six-part manifesto about ministry in the mainline context in the twenty-first century. It is written for church leaders, lay and clergy. The premise of the book is simple, and many will find it radical. Some may conclude it is hopelessly naïve. My premise is this: that God intends every servant of the Resurrected Christ to be a servant of life. God has called all leaders, lay and clergy together, to lead healthy, *growing* spiritual movements.

Any church can blossom and grow anywhere if it will become healthy enough spiritually and pay attention to the needs, experiences, and sensibilities of those it seeks to serve.

For this reason, I refuse to lead a dying church. And I invite you to refuse the same. I invite you to draw a line in the sand with me. I invite you to declare that, from this moment forward, you refuse to simply go through the motions and play church. You hereby refuse to help your church gracefully into the grave. You hereby refuse to channel your best ministry energy into community or justice endeavors that are detached from your congregation's life and ministry. I invite you to join me in refusing, ever again, to lead a dying church. Toward the end of this book, you will be invited to make such a commitment publicly.

As we shall discover in the pages ahead, this commitment entails six critical choices:

- Choosing life over death
- Choosing community over isolation
- Choosing fun over drudgery
- Choosing bold over mild
- Choosing frontier over fortress
- Choosing now rather than later

It's really that simple: six clear choices that will greatly amplify the impact of our lives and of the churches we lead.

But before we explore these choices, I want to take what may seem like a detour but is in fact central to my understanding of spirited Christian leadership. I want to examine briefly what it means to be an apostle. In the first generation of Christian leaders, there was a group of characters that we call *the apostles* who carried the good news of Jesus into the streets and began to change the world. In our generation, it is still apostles who carry the flag of the Christian movement. Living churches have a higher proportion of leaders who are apostles than do dying churches.

Apostles refuse to preside over dying churches.

APOSTOLIC LEADERSHIP

"Always dreamed that I'd be an apostle, knew that I would make it if I tried." Those lyrics by Tim Rice from *Jesus Christ Superstar* first brought the term *apostle* to my young consciousness. There are several different ways that Christian groups understand the term. Some reserve the term *apostle* for those persons who were first-hand witnesses to the resurrected Christ. In these churches the only apostles you may ever see are the flannel board variety in children's Sunday school. Other congregations actually *have* an apostle in residence, typically a preacher, often the pastor, who performs a defined function just as the treasurer would. I do not usually think of an apostle in such structural ways, as a role to be played only by certain people. I think of *apostle* as a mode of being that many persons experience in varying degrees.

Because the word literally means "one who is sent," I define an apostle as any leader who:

- has had *a living experience of meeting Christ* somewhere, somehow, and who then, out of that experience,

- moves with a sense that that he or she is chosen, *is sent* out in life to share something of *eternal value* with the world, and who
- *partners with others* of similar faith and experience in that endeavor.

Many apostles make their living in a secular vocation all of their lives. For other apostles, the mission so consumes their time and energy that keeping another day job is not practical. This mission often drives apostles to the remote corners of their society and to the edges of society's settled assumptions. By both their *passion* and their sheer *audacity*, you can spot them.

Some apostles come off looking cocky because of this. Such hubris is not inevitable for apostolic persons, but it is certainly a danger. Nonapostolic pastors sometimes find apostolic types annoying, too intense, even occasionally suffering from illusions of grandeur. Apostolic pastors often find the others boring. Eyes roll on both sides.

Most mainline churches are a bit unsure what to do with passionate apostolic pastors or laity. This should be no surprise. Mainline faith communities have become a very settled people. Apostles are anything but settled. They have fire in their bellies precisely because when they met Jesus, they got unsettled!

As a group, we mainline pastors tend more to being caretakers and managers of the status quo than to being apostles. We are often driven by the motivation to *help* others—but we seldom believe we have something that can *save* others. And if we did once believe that, chances are we've allowed our seminary training, our ministry peers, our denominational bosses, and the big chieftains in the churches we serve to cure us of that viewpoint. Most of us gave up trying to save the world years ago. This *giving up* goes to the heart of the malaise that now pervades our churches.

Apostolic laity will often grow frustrated because of the lack of urgency or ministry passion expressed by their pastor or other leaders in their church. In response to this frustration they may throw their energy into parachurch organizations, mission projects beyond their local church, or they may leave for a church more in tune with the way they are wired. Sometimes they just quit organized religion altogether.

The quintessential apostle was, of course, a fellow named Paul. Paul was *driven* by God's Spirit down dusty highways all over the Roman Empire in the first century. He was *obsessed* with his mission, obsessed to the point that he likely struggled in his family relationships. His experience of the Living Christ burned in his soul, as did his mission of sharing and living out the good news of Christ, as he understood it. Not even imprisonment could stop him; when he was incarcerated, Paul simply changed his strategy from obsessive traveling to obsessive letter writing.

A more recent character with some parallels to the Apostle Paul was Martin Luther King Jr. The way King framed his mission was somewhat different than Paul; after all, King was applying the Christian good news in a radically different context. But Paul's same sense of passion and conviction that he was sent from God was evident in King and in a whole litany of other characters, male and female, sprinkled across the centuries.

The Apostle Paul's limited vision on how to apply the Christian good news to various social questions has been well spotlighted for several generations now in the mainline churches—to the point that many of us have been basically ignoring him for years in our preaching. (Apostles aren't smarter or morally superior to the rest of the population—they all have their blind sides, even Paul). Martin Luther King Jr.'s troubling personal issues and ethical lapses have been leaking out steadily into the press over the last decade. Yet we haven't been ignoring him. And we likewise ignore Paul at our church's peril.

Most apostolic leaders are not nearly so famous.

Jim Griffith, the most knowledgeable person I know on the subject of new church development in North America, tells me that new church pastors more often succeed in gathering and launching a church if they have certain leadership tendencies, tendencies that he would label *apostolic*. Such apostolic characteristics would include (and I am expanding Jim's list):

- A clear personal experience (often over time) of the Risen Christ that has become the foundation for everything else one does in life.
- Attraction toward friends and relationships on the edge of conventional church circles and often far beyond.
- A clear, and often amazingly simple, sense of mission.
- The passionate conviction that we offer something that will renew human lives and communities.
- The belief that God sent us to this particular place in this particular moment.
- A keen awareness of the ways that organized religion has stopped short of living out the Christian good news faithfully and/or effectively.
- A determination to clear some new territory—to push the church to new places and to new people.
- Boredom with unchanging routine and maintenance tasks.

- Energy discovered in short-term challenges and sprints rather than marathons.

- The capacity to communicate our spiritual experience and vision winsomely to others, so that they are persuaded to jump aboard the bandwagon.

A helpful book edited by Stan Wood entitled *Extraordinary Leaders in Extraordinary Times* documents a landmark study of effective new church pastors in several of the mainline groups. The findings confirm what several of us have been observing for years—these are not business-as-usual pastors. Concerning the apostolic passion that we are describing, Wood writes, "How such passion comes to exist is a holy mystery that is linked to the graciousness of the Holy Spirit working within the human heart."[4]

Of all the findings documented in this study, I was most impressed with the observation that these extraordinary pastors are likely to have led at least one other adult to make a commitment in Christ in the last ninety days.[5] This would amount to four persons a year. Or forty in a decade, or one hundred and sixty persons directly and personally led to faith in Christ over a forty-year pastoral ministry. And again, these were not fundamentalist pastors studied! There are plenty of pastors among us who do not personally lead one adult to new faith in Christ in a decade.

The preceding list of characteristics makes no reference to left, right, or middle theological positions. And yet, liberal

---

4. H. Stanley Wood, "The Tier-One Characteristics of an Extraordinary New-Church Development Pastor," an essay contained in *Extraordinary Leaders in Extraordinary Times: Unadorned Clay Pot Messengers*, vol. 1, ed. H. Stanley Wood (Grand Rapids: Eerdmans, 2006), 30.
5. Ibid., 82.

Protestant denominations have relatively few clergy who could be described like this. We on the left are usually oriented toward different emphases and goals besides growing churches and leading people to faith in Christ. We may have adopted a particular social issue as the centerpiece of our witness. On a global stage, some pastors may work hard educating others about the need for a Palestinian homeland or about ways of slowing the destruction of the earth's rainforests. On a local stage, we may work for the creation of affordable housing and just working conditions for the poor. These are each holy tasks; but if we are not creating more disciples to follow Jesus and serve humanity in these respects, our efforts will dry up in coming years—because we will dry up. It is sad to imagine a world devoid of such Christian social witness. Yet if our churches cannot reproduce disciples, we could inadvertently bequeath such a world to our grandchildren.

I have a colleague who directs new church development in a major metropolitan area for a mainline liberal denomination. His judicatory has significant financial and leadership resources, but they cannot complete a successful new church start to save their lives. They are genuinely perplexed about this. I believe the main reason for their lack of success is that they have very few apostolic persons in the ranks of their clergy, few ready to undertake the task of new church development. The kinds of leaders that they need to succeed in such ministry assignments have not often been attracted into pastoral ministry in these faith communities, at least not lately. (In such a situation, a denomination may wish to consider pairing apostolic laity with their best clergy in teams for the task of new church development.)

This same metropolitan area contains some of the fastest growing congregations in the nation, almost all of which are independent evangelical churches, started in the last thirty years by apostolic leaders. Such churches more often nurture and affirm these kinds of leaders. It is mostly evangelical churches that choose to mother new congregations and to send effective leaders out to guide them. We should not, therefore, be surprised that most of the new churches rising on the American landscape are right of center theologically. If we mainliners in the middle and on the left cannot match this energy for evangelism in our own style, the implications for the future of American religion are plain—our flavor of Christianity will be largely missing from the options available in most communities. Already this is happening in many places.

Let me be very clear: *apostolic leaders come in varied theological flavors!* Much of the time, mainline denominations simply do not know what to do with such leaders anymore. Consequently, many of our more liberal/progressive apostles find other arenas, beyond church, in which to pursue their passions for changing the world. A good number of the apostolic pastors who do emerge in the mainline churches were in fact raised in more evangelical denominations or evangelical corners of the mainline denominations—in an environment where often they experienced their call to ministry. Over the years, they matured and outgrew certain perspectives, and eventually they emerged as effective leaders with more liberal groups.

The first characteristic of apostolic leaders that I listed is related to their experience of Christ. I do not want to gloss over that, as if to imply that you can be solid on the other bullet points and get by. Being strong on 80 percent of the characteristics is not good enough. *There simply are no apostles who haven't met Christ personally, somewhere, somehow.*

What does it look like for a mainline leader to meet Christ? It is more than likely different than evangelical concepts of "accepting Christ."

One theologically liberal pastor was taken aback when I told her she was an apostolic leader. She asked me what I meant, and I said something similar to what I have written above. She replied that she had never had a Damascus Road experience with Jesus. I responded, "So what? You still met Christ somewhere. It shows, powerfully." She reflected for a time, and then shared this:

> I think it was one Christmas morning, after spending my Christmas Eve in worship and then (all night) at the homeless shelter in the (church) basement. One of the homeless guys had fallen asleep on the floor next to the Christmas tree. He looked to be waiting for Santa. But I think he was waiting for Jesus. I saw Jesus often, spending the night in that shelter once a month.

She didn't walk down the aisle and fill out a card for the prayer team at the local megachurch, but she had met the Risen Christ all the same—and such an encounter is more than enough to begin a lifelong process of growth and to transform the nature of one's leadership.

A few months after this, I saw Jesus with my own eyes on the subway in Washington D.C., in the form of a blind, paraplegic woman being led on wheels by a yellow Labrador retriever through throngs of strangers she could not see. You may say, "That was not the Risen Christ, just a courageous young woman," but this would be a matter of faith perspective. Seeing her empowered me for weeks after that through some rather difficult decisions, challenges directly related to my obedience to Christ's Great Commission. I will never forget the holiness of that moment.

I want to assume that you've met Christ along your life's journey or you would not be in Christian ministry. However, I realize that this is not a safe assumption. If you do not have a personal experience with Jesus of some sort (and I use this language very intentionally), this book may be frustrating for you. Of course, apostolic leadership is more than vital spirituality. But it builds on that and moves out from that. Without this foundation of spiritual experience, all the good choices in the world will yield little joy in your life, and limited effectiveness. If you've met Christ in a way that truly changed you, then there is nothing in the pages ahead that is not doable for you.

The range of theological beliefs among apostles is breathtaking. One apostle may take the Bible very literally, another quite metaphorically. One may believe that anyone who doesn't accept Christ as Savior in a certain manner will go to hell after death. Another may believe that in the end, God will round up all her stray children. One apostle may speak in tongues and encourage others to exercise that gift. Another may not be comfortable going anywhere near that topic. One apostle may be radically inclusive of diverse people as they round up disciples; another may be really uncomfortable with certain population groups.

The urgency that propels apostles forward isn't necessarily a mania to prevent people from going to hell after death. Sometimes it is just that. Other times it is an urgency to prevent people from living in hell in this life—or to build a coalition of allies who are determined to give their lives to make this world a more just and gentle place, more reflective of the realm of God. Sometimes the apostle's urgency is simply to love others as he or she has so powerfully been loved.

Among the growing congregations in the dying denominations, there are common themes. The evangelical renegade congregations[6] often grow, especially in suburbia. Another set of renegade churches that we may find in the net growth column are those churches who have designated themselves as "open and affirming" of all persons, regardless of sexual orientation. It is common to find urban congregations that had been declining and drifting for decades turning around and beginning to thrive again, about the time they chose to be officially "open and affirming."

Growing churches tend to share the following things in common, even when they are theological polar opposites:

- These churches are each more likely to team up with apostles as their pastoral leaders than are other congregations.

- They demonstrate genuine interest in taking risks to reach the people in their communities who are not currently served well by the church.

- They are willing to adjust and change in at least a few key respects (varying vastly from church to church) in order to reach a changing population.

- They hold to sets of core beliefs and values that become sacrosanct within their fellowship, and become nonnegotiable. Though these core beliefs and values may vary widely from one church to the next, growing churches generally do not attempt to be all things to all

6. By renegade, I mean to say that some congregations see themselves as distinctive within their denomination, differing from the majority in one respect or another. We should never assume that just because a congregation marches to a slightly different drumbeat that they love their denominational connection less or feel disloyal to that connection.

people. There always remains some set of persons who will be offended, persons who would clearly be happier participating in another church.

Their rationale for evangelism varies considerably; but the fact remains that most growing churches believe in evangelism—at least to the degree that *they want new people in their ranks.* They want others to discover the spiritual blessings that they have discovered. They want to share their church with strangers and newcomers, many of whom have different cultural instincts and values. *Leaders in such churches care more about everyone coming to know Christ than they care about keeping their churches small enough so that they can know everyone.*[7] It is no wonder, then, that apostolic pastors gravitate toward such churches.

If you are a mainline pastor and you resonate with the bulleted points listed a few pages back that define what makes an apostle, there is at least a chance that you have found a rare place in your denomination where you can be the leader God created you to be! In that case, your ministry is likely thriving, and your denominational office thanks you for your financial support! Very possibly, however, if you are an apostle in a mainline church, you have not found a place to exercise your calling and, as a result, you may be growing bored and frustrated in ministry. You may feel as if no one in your tribe understands you. Apostles in mainline churches sometimes come to believe that they made a wrong career choice.

If you are a layperson and you resonate with the bulleted points, I hope you have found a local church that wants to

---

7. This is a distinction that my friend Bill Easum has used often; I am not sure who coined it.

live and thrive and risk in ministry. If your church is not there yet, you have some prayerful discernment to do about where your life should best be spent—pushing for change in a resistant church system or relocating to a congregational context where you can make the difference God wants to make through you.

If you are a mainline pastor and you do *not* resonate with the bulleted points from a few pages back, you may be well-loved by your tribe but you are probably also underachieving in ministry. Deep in your heart, you know something is not right, that you are tending a slowly sinking ship—and so you, too, may be growing bored and frustrated in ministry. You may not be quite as naturally wired for apostolic leadership as another person, but you are probably more capable of such than you are aware. Don't sell yourself short.

If you are a layperson in a mainline church and you do not resonate with the material that you are reading so far, this short book may be a tough read for you. But it is a short book, and I invite you to hang in there for a couple of hours before assuming that you know where this conversation is going. It may very well surprise you, and finally resonate with some of your core convictions.

Why?

Because I can find no grounds, biblical or otherwise, for assuming that some leaders are born apostles and others aren't. Any leader who has a living experience with Christ can make apostolic choices; any leader can claim apostolic values. *Apostle* is not a Myers-Briggs personality category where "some are and some are not." In fact, experience has persuaded me that even specified leader/personality types as defined by standardized instruments (such as the Myers-Briggs or DISC personality assessments) are dynamic and malleable over time, varying in large part upon one's experience, training, and values. Leadership style certainly is not doled out predetermined from heaven like lottery numbers.

There *is* such a thing as a spiritual gift—we are gifted differently in life. But *if* our faith community has perceived in us the gift of spiritual leadership *and* we have met the Risen Christ, *then* there is no reason for us not to act like an apostle. And to lead like one!

The mainline churches in North America are dying for lack of apostolic leaders. If the only apostle one ever meets at the place you call church is of the flannel board variety, I can say with near certainty—your church is dying, or soon will be.

The remainder of this book unpacks six apostolic choices that will serve to further the transformation that began as you met the Living Christ. These choices will transform you, and in turn, transform the churches and the communities you serve.

A free study guide for this book is available online at www.epicentergroup.org. It is designed for groups in local churches as well as for groups of leaders from multiple churches in which each person is reading the book. The guide is available in both four-session and six-session formats. It is much easier to apply the principles contained in *I Refuse to Lead a Dying Church!* when a community of leaders in a congregation is together in conversation.

1   CHOOSING LIFE OVER DEATH

From the earliest years of my faith exploration, the words of German theologian Jürgen Moltmann have haunted me:

> Where Jesus is, there is life. There is abundant life, vigorous life, loved life and eternal life. There is life-before-death. I find it deeply disturbing and unsettling whenever I think about how we have become accustomed to death—to the death of the soul, to death on the street, to death through violence—to death-before-life.[8]

To his list I'm compelled to add how disturbed and unsettled I feel whenever I think about how accustomed we have become to the death of the church.

8. Jürgen Moltmann, *The Passion for Life: A Messianic Lifestyle*, trans. M. Douglas Meeks (Philadelphia: Fortress Press, 1977), 19.

I began pastoral ministry in the Cascade Mountains of Washington state. It was a summer assignment, nothing more—fourteen short weeks. I was a student exploring God's call on my life, looking for a summer mission experience in which to test and discover how God had gifted me for life. What happened was this: one night in the spring of my first year in college, I received one of those remarkable phone calls where someone says, "We have a job for you!" It was a judicatory executive from the Pacific Northwest calling to invite me to serve as the interim pastor of a church that had, in fact, just officially closed. The little church building sat at the central traffic light in the heart of a thriving mountain community. Despite an enviable location, the congregation had dwindled to seven active members, two of whom were the former pastor and his wife. Just before I arrived for my summer adventure, as the church closed, they ceded all assets to a growing church in nearby Wenatchee. The Wenatchee church desired to keep the doors open in the mountain church but had little money to invest. They could not have found a better buy than me. I required simply room and board in exchange for the adventure of working sixty hours a week to jump-start ministry in a place where it had died. Inadvertently, in this project, the Wenatchee church became a multisite congregation two decades before the multisite church movement gained momentum in America. My job was to lead services at the mountain campus as they regrouped under new management. I was not quite nineteen years old.

On my first Sunday, we had eleven persons present. I was so nervous about having to lead a worship service that I physically shook for some time afterwards. The seventeen-year-old kid they sent me to lead the music was even more of a wreck than I was. The fact that anyone came back the next week is a wonder. But I expected no less. I could not imagine any reason why this church—or any church—should fail to thrive, despite whatever had happened before I got to town.

In fact, the people did come back, a few more each week. On any given Sunday, one or two would venture up the mountain from Wenatchee to monitor what was going on; another three or four tourists would wander in. The rest of the folks were local.

Over the fourteen weeks, armed with a trusty map and a stack of crude brochures, I took it upon myself to visit every home in this community of fifteen hundred people. I went door to door. I did not consult any experts to determine what percentage of favorable response I would likely receive. I just started walking. I walked in on more than one family fight and on several naturists who answered the door without clothes on. I kept those visits brief. At some doorsteps, we talked theology. At other places, people fed me refreshments. If some folks weren't too keen on organized religion, I invited them to the community cinema we ran in the church basement on Friday evenings—reel-to-reel Disney films and free popcorn.

On each of the last three Sundays that summer, we had more than forty persons at worship. We served a couple dozen children in Vacation Bible School. Three persons professed faith in Christ that summer. I turned nineteen, decided to change my major, and descended that mountain embracing pastoral ministry as my life calling.

And the church lived.

At that point in my life, I had never read a church leadership book or a book on family systems and dysfunctions; so I had not yet been taught all the reasons why my naïve efforts should have failed. Furthermore, I am certain that my sermons were meandering, repetitive, and tedious. I mean, I was still a teenager. The building had no air conditioning, and the church house got pretty warm in July. But I expected the church to thrive, and it did. I also hit the streets and worked my tail off that summer—and I prayed like crazy. Every morning at 5 o'clock I would go walking with God down the rural lane where I stayed. I refused to lead a dying church, and God honored my refusal. God blessed both the community and our little church.

Since those long-ago days I've learned that such turnaround efforts are more likely to work when:

- The church has dwindled to the point of desperation.
- A healthier church or other outside authority takes over management, so that the old decision-making structures are suspended.
- The leader takes the time to hit the streets and purposefully network in the community.
- A *lot* of praying occurs.
- Beyond the initial splash, the leader changes gears slightly and begins to invest her or his time mentoring other leaders in the congregation.

Had I transferred to a college in Washington and continued serving there, the old-timers in the church might have perceived me as more of a threat. Had they been more threatened, I probably would have encountered more direct opposition to the decisions and practices necessary to serve that community effectively.

The number one reason I observe that turnaround efforts fail is that certain controllers in the dying church try to set up a power tug-of-war with the new leader. This happens just short of 100 percent of the time. In stagnant and dying churches, the members usually turn inward and become a bit selfish in what they expect of the church; decisions are made based upon what is most convenient and comfortable for the church members rather than what is expedient in effectively serving the community people.

The second most common reason that turnaround efforts fail is that the new leader fails to build a broad enough alliance for the changes she or he begins pursuing. In a recent interview between Bill Hybels and *Good to Great* author Jim Collins, Collins observed that great pastors are more like senators than presidents.[9] Our best power is realized in our ability to forge the necessary coalitions to get things done; the best pastors do not rule by fiat. I observe that new pastors fail to build the coalitions they need about 75 percent of the time. Often the most helpful persons to partner with are inactive members: community leaders, movers and shakers, who have grown bored or frustrated with their church over the years and who may have turned their energy toward other good projects in the community. They may have become disconnected entirely from the official leadership structure and now seldom attend worship. Discovering these persons and nurturing relationships with them may reactivate their interest and energy—and unleash miracles for your church.

Because of these two realities (lay controllers and failure of pastors to build strategic coalitions), most dying churches do not turn around. However, wherever the pastor plays her or his

---

9. The Leadership Summit, sponsored by the Willow Creek Association, broadcast to varied sites around the United States, August 11, 2006.

hand well, gently inviting partnership and collaboration with others, and trusting God, miracles usually happen. Church is, after all, God's business. We pastors are just the front people for what God is up to—and when we get our own egos and neediness out of the way, we give God space to work.

One way or another, we leaders must choose life for the churches we lead.

We then must invite a coalition of partners who will also choose life over death.

Now, please note that in many dying and stagnant churches, the majority of the remaining members will not be prepared to choose life. As Jesus discovered in Nazareth a few years back, sometimes a place isn't ready for the ministry we have to offer—and, in such cases, we may be wise to just ease on down the road before they throw us off a cliff.

Prayer will usually dislodge a few of the stubborn folks and get them on board. But many will likely choose to continue sitting in the same pew, socializing with the same cronies, expecting the same worship services and the same pastoral care (for themselves). *More often than not, the would-be turnaround pastor will arrive to cast a ministry vision and discover only a few bright eyes in the room*—only a few folks who "get it" or who even want to get it. If you find yourself in such a place, I urge you to take names. Keep a list of the bright-eyed people, the people who are energized by the thought of their church living and thriving in ministry with a new set of people. Work to grow that list. (And if you can't grow that group, then move on to a place where you can!)

One new pastor convened a dozen inactive church members at a banquet room in town, persons all rumored to be quite wealthy. He cast his ministry vision with them and invited them to invest in it. Most of these people had demonstrated significant leadership and wisdom in their secular endeavors. He told them, "I need you!" Several of the members were reactivated, and more than half gave generously to a new ministry development fund. And their previously dying church turned the corner toward life.

Another new pastor ran a series of dessert gatherings at her home for various church groups, charming the socks off her would-be detractors. She knew that she was at her best when she was hosting a party in her home. So she chose that setting to build relationships with key groups: the choir and a couple of adult Sunday school classes in particular. In each gathering, she listened and observed. Then with gentleness and with intentional use of the same language that others had used in expressing their hopes and dreams to her, she began to cast a vision. Within a few months, attendance and giving in her church had leapt to record levels, as the core constituency rallied around the hospitality that their new pastor had extended *toward them.*

Grow the list of vision shareholders—both inside the church membership and beyond it! Keep a roll. This roll is your real church roll. I cannot overstate how important it is that you reframe your ministry toward this roll of living disciples rather than toward the larger roll of accumulated names that have, for whatever reasons, been added to the church over the last seventy years. The bright-eyed people form the green shoot poking its way to life from what appeared to be a dead tree. Growing this new shoot is your main task as a turnaround leader. This shoot, these people are the living church you are called by God to lead.

Spend time developing these people. Study the Scriptures with them. Play with them. Pray with them. Laugh with them. Eat with them. Dream with them. Hit the streets with them.

Encourage them to use their gifts and passions for the sake of the reign of God. Teach them how to leverage what is fun for them as a mission to the community.

You are looking for people in whom spiritual life is evident in your first weeks in this new place. And you are looking for big thinkers and natural leaders wherever you can find them in the community. Wherever you find life, offer your pastoral presence and your leadership to that. *Tend primarily to what is living, not to what is passing away.*

As you grow the roll of people who get it and who choose life, do not be discouraged if the *official* church roll continues to shrink. Whatever the bishop or the pastor search committee chooses to believe, an apostolic leader is not here to pastor the whole church roll. You will offer some pastoral care to the larger group, but your assignment is to lead a living church. That living church certainly entails a much shorter roster of members than whatever you print up in the church phone directory, along with some folks who are not yet members but could be. Therefore, as a leader who chooses life for your church, you are probably going to begin keeping score differently than the typical pastor or the judicatory executives. *Choosing life means reframing the playing field for your ministry in a way that enables you to concentrate on what is living and thriving, and to pastor that.*

Ken Callahan tells of a dying church where several of the members were master gardeners—and yet the churchyard was knee high in weeds. He invited them to turn their energy for flowers on the churchyard, so that soon that church would be known about town as the church with the incredible flowerbed. That accomplishment felt so good that they then began to look for other high-visibility spots about town that needed great flowers. Others joined in. Eventually, that church had half a dozen "garden groups" sharing faith and life together. The very act of planting life all around town became an apt metaphor for what happened in their church. They chose life. Measuring ministry growth and life in such a church is tricky—but I would guess that success here has a lot to do with the expanding number of participants in garden groups, especially the newcomers. Life here has almost nothing to do with the official number of names on the church roll.

As you grow your circle of people who choose life, I would encourage you to offer just enough quality pastoral care to the rest of the group to fend off a significant spike in the complaining. Reserve your best time investment for the people who choose life. It may take two or three years for your visionary core to become a formidable force, but at about the time when the controllers perceive that real change is afoot, you will be in a much stronger position to ride through the turbulence if you have built a team around you who share a passion for ministry.

If we are not focused on growing a new thing in an old place, it is very easy to become simply a caretaker of a church in decline. More often than not, folks begin to expect this of us. After several years ministering to decline, it begins to change us, to warp us. We can become ministers of death rather than life. Our major expenditures of time go toward tinkering with institutional and pastoral concerns in order to manage the decline. Our fund-raising efforts go largely to integrate the latest technology and architectural design into a house largely empty of people under the age of forty. Or we may simply pour ourselves into another mission project, perhaps related to an issue of social justice in a faraway place—and do nothing to lead *the church* God has sent us to lead.

We are invited to choose life, to be servants of life. We are invited to refuse, ever again, to be servants of death. Does this mean that there are certain places where we refuse to go if the bishop sends us there or God calls us there? Not at all! It may mean that we need to let the powers-that-be know that if we accept the assignment to serve as pastor in a dying situation, we will not go in with a modest approach. In other words: Fair warning, bishop! Fair warning, pastor search committee! You may have people on your doorstep six months after I arrive demanding that you deliver them of me! I am delighted to serve here, but be warned in advance, I choose life! *I refuse to lead a dying church!* I promise to be kind in my approach, but I will, by design, spend . . .

- Less time in pastoral care of accumulated membership
- More time building bridges in the community
- Less time in pointless meetings
- More time developing the leaders that will be taking the church into its future.

We are called to choose life. But, as we can see, this choice leads to some other choices—first of all, about the way we spend our time. In the chapters ahead, we will discover five other big choices that flow from our choice to be servants of life.

2 CHOOSING COMMUNITY OVER ISOLATION

One of the recent bromides being passed around to comfort leaders of faith communities in decline is the notion that people are somehow less civic-minded today than in times past, that they are withdrawing into a more self-centered world. People used to join churches, we are told, as part of their community affiliation, along with their lodge or fraternal order. Each of these institutions is now dealing with aging membership. I want to be clear about what I think of this notion that people are somehow withdrawing from the public arena into a private world. Read my lips:

B-U-N-K.

First, people are as starved for meaningful community today as at any other time in human history. Some things just come with being human. Churches that provide meaningful community typically pack out their house and often return folks in large numbers to the world in various forms of community service.

Second, people are constantly changing the ways that they express their need for social connection and for investment in others. Technology has made it possible for folks to reach out beyond their immediate geographical territory to connect with folks with whom they share affinities.

Third, today almost no one will remain loyal to any church or organization unless they perceive that it works for them. In a world of such wonderful choices, there is simply no reason anymore for any of us to waste our time on enterprises that we perceive as boring or irrelevant. There are too many other good things to do out there! A recent study of the evolving attitudes of college students from freshman to senior years discovered that, with each year, their interest in exploring life's spiritual dimension increases. Yet, over the same time span, their sense that organized religion is relevant to that exploration steadily diminishes. Church, as we know it, simply doesn't work for most young adults. It is neither the quest for spirituality nor for authentic community that turns this generation off. Rather, they are exasperated by the wearisome, irrelevant institutional expressions of spirituality and community.

Fourth, each new generation varies in social attitudes, in dress, in cars, in leisure pursuits from the older generations. Many institutions that once were effective in helping people find community are less than enthusiastic about accommodating these changes in order to offer a venue for meaningful community to new generations of people.

In my experience of mainline faith communities in America, they are sometimes bastions of isolation, not places of thriving community. Granted, there are tiny circles of closed community in most churches—small groups of folks who have gathered for years to quilt or to study. But typically, a very small number of the total participants in mainline churches share in such community. Here is what I often see in our established churches:

- People scattered across a worship space that is too big for the crowd present, sitting in isolation from one another.

- No systematic design for contacting or connecting with people when they drop out of worship participation for more than a couple weeks, feeding the common perception that "nobody gives a damn whether I show up or not."

- A nice coffee time after the service, but a lack of settings where people move beyond small talk to share real hurts and hopes with one another.

- Fortress-like buildings erected in another era by people that used to live in the neighborhood, but who either died or moved somewhere else—so that the building now functions as an alien and intimidating presence in the new neighborhood, typically locked up 165 hours a week (a theme we explore in depth in chapter 5).

- Ministries to the poor often offered at arms-length distance from the people served. We do not design such ministry as part of a larger strategy of relationship building that will draw the neighbors and us together in partnership and authentic spiritual community.

In such a reality, it is silly for us to delude ourselves with the notion that people are dropping out because they are somehow less community-minded. They are more likely leaving to look for community somewhere else where they think they have a better shot at finding it! And, of course, the place where they are looking may or may not be another church. Some people find far more authentic community at their neighborhood karaoke bar than they would ever find in their neighborhood church.

If, as a church leader, you dare to choose community over isolation, there are two key aspects of this choice—one is your church's relationship to the wider community around it. The other is the quality of the community that exists within the church itself. If you are like most mainline church leaders, you will pour more enthusiasm into the first concern than you will into the latter. If your church is very extroverted, these concerns will blur together a bit. (And that's okay!) For our purposes here, we will examine each issue separately.

RELATIONSHIP TO OUTSIDE COMMUNITY

First, let's think about your church's relationship to its wider community.

Thriving churches choose to pour themselves out in service to the communities of people that live beyond their walls and membership lists. Choosing community over isolation first of all means choosing to spend more of your time as a leader connecting with the wider community of people God intends for your church to serve. Second, it means leading your church to *think community* and embrace your community in all you do. This is a major theme in my previous books.[10]

It is very hard for you to lead your church beyond community isolation if you choose isolation for yourself. Offices and computers are great assets in our work when they are

10. *Fling Open the Doors: Giving Your Church Away to the Community* (Nashville: Abingdon Press, 2002) and *Healing Spiritual Amnesia: Remembering What It Means to Be the Church* (Nashville: Abingdon Press, 2004).

used in measured doses of time. In truth, the most important thing you can do at the office is pray . . . and more often than not, I have walked down the hall to the sanctuary or out onto the street even to do that. Jesus gave quality time for prayer in his daily routine. But then he usually pushed himself out the door and down the road into the community. *The most effective pastors turn off their computers, grab their cell phones and leave their offices for a meaningful period of time each day to interact purposefully with others in the community.*

In days past, joining a community club like Rotary or Kiwanis often helped a leader form helpful relationships in the community. In some places, such participation may still be helpful. However, if you are limited in your time—and most of us are—you want to find ways that you can form relationships with persons who are reflective of the larger community your church needs to serve and to disciple. Hopeful possibilities for community connections include the following:

- Offer to serve as volunteer chaplain for a fire station.
- Offer to serve as volunteer chaplain for a police precinct.
- Offer to serve as a mentor in the local schools and/or as a volunteer chaplain for teachers and staff.
- Offer to use a specific skill or interest as a volunteer in the school system, such as announcing at ballgames or coaching the debate team.
- Offer to serve as a pastor on-call for a nearby funeral home, specifically for local families who have no church or pastor.
- Simply become a regular fixture at a local coffee house or fitness club. (If they have an area there that can be closed

off from the main traffic, see if your church can hold occasional events on their premises, and save on your church's utility bill in the process.)

- If there is a self-help group meeting in your church facility and it holds open meetings, check with the leaders to see if it would be okay for you to drop in occasionally to encourage folks in their recovery and to let them see that you are an approachable, nonjudgmental person. If you are a recovering person yourself, all the better!

- Make a deal that you will meet any member for lunch if that person will arrange to bring a work colleague or other friend along so you can meet him or her as well. Go to their workplace first prior to lunch—meet them there and then you can venture to your chosen lunch spot together. Always keep your eyes open for opportunities to set up short-term groups in such work places—perhaps to teach a popular book over three weeks.

In any of the preceding connections that open up for you, be sure to invite your church to partner with you *somehow* in the relationship. For example, the church can adopt specific teachers or firefighters to pray for by name; you can bring meals to them; you can partner with them in their mission of serving others as special needs become apparent that they are not equipped to handle. You can even honor them occasionally at a church service, special picnic, or other community event.

As the years pass by and your church grows, you, as a pastor-leader, will need to manage your time very carefully. You will want to be extremely selective in your community investments, choosing the types of activities that have proven to be most fruitful for helping community people get connected to your church. Meanwhile, if you approach community involvement from a team orientation, you will have established several opportunities for church folks to stay invested on a variety of fronts, blessing community people, sharing faith, and making lots of friends for the church.

As your church develops relationships with more and more people from the community around it, you will take specific actions to create a more hospitable zone for community people to enter. You will work to upgrade the hospitality systems on Sundays and at other times when you are inviting community people onto your turf. You may wish to adopt a statement of welcome to specific people groups who often wonder if they are truly welcome. Non-English-speaking groups, gay persons, and spiritual seekers are examples of such groups. In addition, you will probably develop new worship services that use music and liturgical forms that are more effective with the people you are trying to reach. These are all efforts that stem from a leader's (and a church's) decision to choose community.

RELATIONSHIP TO COMMUNITY WITHIN

But there is another, equally critical side of choosing community and that involves choosing a deeper, more authentic experience of community *within* a church's fellowship. It is the choice to move intentionally closer to the type of life sharing described in Acts 2:42–46:

> They devoted themselves to the apostles' teaching and fellowship, to the breaking of bread and the prayers. Awe came upon everyone, because many wonders and signs were being done by the apostles. All who believed were together and had all things in common; they would sell their possessions and goods and distribute

the proceeds to all, as any had need. Day by day, as they spent much time together in the temple, they broke bread at home and ate their food with glad and generous hearts, praising God and having the goodwill of all the people. And day by day the Lord added to their number those who were being saved.

It's hard enough work building solid connectedness with the world beyond your walls. But, in the mainline churches, that is often easier than raising the level of authentic community within the church itself. Some of you will be tempted to bypass the next few pages and skip on to chapter 3. Plenty of churches in your denomination may appear to be thriving simply off a really magnetic worship service. But I want you to know that most of those churches are simply scratching the surface of what they could do and become if they were more intentional about rediscovering the magic of Acts 2.

In my work with new church starts, we take the practices that are common to thriving new churches in America and proscribe them for the churches we are seeking to birth. One practice that sets thriving new churches apart from the pack is the creation and nurture of a dynamic network of small groups within most of those new churches. These small groups typically meet in homes. They usually function as the basic building blocks of pastoral care, fellowship, and spiritual formation. So when a participant in the church comes on tough times, it is the fellow small group members, rather than the church's pastor, who offer the front line of care and support. We know such groups work, because thousands of churches around the world have experienced the power of such community.

But when we get a group of mainline American church folks together at the beginning of the process of birthing a new congregation, they typically are disinterested in home groups. They want to have a worship service instead. We tell them that we will start with relational groups, which will grow and multiply for several months before we launch a worship service, but this idea often goes right over their heads. Many grow disinterested in the project—and this is not a bad thing in the short term because we do not want typical church people to subvert the success of a new church! Each time that I work with an emerging church that chooses to take a shortcut around the hard work of building authentic community via small groups, I later wish that I had pushed them harder in this arena. In every *thriving* new church start with which I have worked, much energy has been devoted to community-building. Conversely, in every *failed* new church start with which I have worked, I believe the church would have thrived if only the project leadership had been radically committed to choosing community—in *both* of the respects that we are discussing, outside the church and within.

We know three things: 1) that small groups work, and 2) that they are powerful forces for spiritual life in the churches that depend upon them. We also know 3) that the people who have been hanging out in traditional churches often have major resistance to such groups—and even when they consent to join a group, the group may quickly become a closed system because they either will not invite their friends or they complain, inexplicably, that they cannot get anyone to come to their homes.

I ask them if people come to their home when invited to a party. They will tell me yes. I then say, "Your home group is a party." They respond with a blank stare. I have concluded that this is learned behavior. We have trained people to behave this way. There is simply no other cogent explanation about why something that is so effective and works so well in so many places finds such resistance among many long-time church people.

We have to help people who were raised in a culture of spiritual isolation to face and change their long-learned habits and fears. Fewer than half of your folks may go with you at first. But community is essential to a thriving church! So, as you choose community, I ask you in all earnestness—please do not back off the intentional development of relational groups! You may have to innovate in terms of how to do such group-work in your unique setting, but *do not* let your folks off the hook!

You will hear some pastors say, "Small groups don't work." The real message beneath those words is, "I have not been willing to work hard enough to lead my people toward the discovery of authentic Christian community in the small group setting." That is all they are saying.

You may experiment with several different ways of doing groups in your setting. One size does not fit all in small group work any more than one size fits all in worship. You can expect the following challenges in trying to adapt the small group models perfected by the evangelical churches to the mainline setting:

- If your church is theologically to the left, you will have fewer easy-to-use study resources for small group settings. Most of the small group resources currently marketed in the local Christian bookstores is very conservative theologically. Some of the more liberal stuff is either so esoteric or so far removed from the personal spiritual journey (dealing exclusively with political and justice issues) that it is not helpful in building up people's faith. Other good resources will have to be adapted for group study. There is a small but steady stream of effective small group resources for moderate and left-of-center churches emerging, including *Living the Questions* and *Companions in Christ*. A lot of great books can be adapted for group use if they touch upon issues that are important to the people you are trying to gather.

- If your church is made up of highly professional, highly paid, highly traveled, highly scheduled people, you will find a good number of folks will respond, at first, by saying they are too busy to commit to such a group. These are the people who try to cram two years of life into one. (I am one of these people, so I can relate. It is difficult for me to take even a once-a-week course at the community college due to the intensity and unpredictability of my work schedule and travel.) For these folks, consider offering a one-time three-hour group experience that is repeated two or three times over the course of a month before the next experience is offered. Participants will then make it their goal to hit one of the three experiences each month and to spend the better part of an evening with a group of fellow seekers.

- There are a lot of folks whose personality type does not lead them toward sitting in a circle in anyone's living room, discussing any topic, let alone religion. They may be most effectively gathered at first around a helping project, where there is little sitting and navel-gazing, but more focus on a task that offers help and hope to others.

- In urban settings especially, the sheer diversity of life experience, faith backgrounds, and cultural roots means that a one-size-fits-all small group strategy probably won't work as well as it would in a semirural or suburban area.

- More of us are snobs than would admit it. After we discover the joy of cross-cultural community, we will ease up and go to just about anyone's house. But when we are just sticking our toe in the water, we will likely not go to anyone's house unless it is someone in our socioeconomic bracket or close to it, *and* unless we are certain that we will know more than one person when we get there. So there is value in creating festive large group events that we can invite friends to attend. In these events newcomers can get a taste of the church, and make a few friends—who in turn can invite them to something more in-depth.

- If people are offered the chance to enroll in a class that meets in the church facility, the chances of them going to a home group drops significantly. If your church has a well-developed network of adult classes held in the church facility, you will discover home groups more difficult to establish than if there are fewer classes in the facility.

None of the preceding obstacles is insurmountable. But if we don't name these challenges right up front, the chances increase that you will grow discouraged when you try to implement a small group system that some church perfected in another city, and it fails to take root after your first effort.

Remember that the goal is to get people connected and in community with others who share common faith and common goals. Small groups are proven as the best means of delivering this kind of community to the most people. *Unless your context proves this to be unworkable, I recommend that you make the home group the norm for your small group ministry.* At the same time, I recommend that you stay open to innovation and variation—doing whatever it takes to connect as many folks as you can in Christian community. One group may meet before work in the back of a McDonalds. Another may form around doing something helpful and productive when they meet—and only sit and talk occasionally to reflect on what God is teaching them in their work. Where people commute across a large region to worship in one place, some groups may need to gather during the time that people are already together; those groups may look and act an awful lot like Sunday school classes.

You certainly should not expect all of your small groups to have identical agendas. Occasionally, you may ask each of the groups to focus on a common theme or even to use a church-wide study resource. But, on most weeks, each group needs to look and act different. Some will be drawn together primarily on the basis of a common hobby or activity that they enjoy pursuing together. Other groups will be drawn together primarily on the basis of a common life-stage and experience (such as being working mothers of preschool children). Still other groups will be drawn together because of a common interest in reading a provocative book on spirituality or because of a passion to do something as a blessing to the community. It is good to encourage such diversity in a small group system.

At the same time, there will need to be some common denominators in all of the small groups. These may vary slightly from one church to another, but common denominators that I would encourage include:

- *Gathering at least twice monthly* (Groups should consider coming together weekly if it is doable; but with e-mail reminders, many groups are able to function well on an every-other-week basis.)
- *Breaking bread together, as often as the group meets.* In Acts 2, sharing meals is the only component of the early

church's life that is mentioned twice. Food, coffee, and table sharing is a nonnegotiable. This is how we naturally open up to one another.

- *Intentionally including new people, as often as the group meets.* If two meetings go by with no new persons in attendance, plan to go out to eat as a group or to gather to watch a ballgame. In short, create a special event that is easy and natural for inviting friends. The point of this special, occasional gathering will be simply to make friends and build new relationships with persons who may then choose to accept your invitation to join you for your regular gatherings to study or to serve.

- *Sitting down together, at least once monthly.* Reflect on what God is teaching us in our lives, and open a Bible. My friend Jim Griffith, a leading coach among new church developers, was the first person I ever heard to offer the somewhat obvious observation that, finally, church leadership involves getting bodies in chairs.

- *Doing something, at least once monthly, to bless others.* The variety of ministry projects is infinite and will vary according to community needs and the gifts/passions of the group members. Some groups may make this the basis of their existence. Other groups will simply go into serving mode on a monthly basis somewhere in the community.

- *Praying for one another and offering appropriate support to each other* through life's challenging moments as well as through life's joys. Someone should voice a prayer every time the group meets. This is critically important so that the group remembers that it is has a spiritual basis, and that God is the center of its life. But a prayer at the group meeting is simply the tip of the iceberg. The most significant praying for others happens on a daily basis. Often, the group will encourage or assign one-on-one prayer partners who lift one another up daily.

If such groups are new to your church's life, you may want to take some time leading and sharing in a group or two with different constituencies. Set up each group to include people from outside the church. Learn what works and what does not work in your setting.

Some churches find that it is helpful to run such groups in cycles or, to use an educational paradigm, in semesters. A church can divide the year into two, three, or four group seasons, with breaks in between. One church may do groups in eight- or nine-week cycles with three-week breaks. You can do four of those in a year. Another church may do groups in twelve-week cycles with a one-month break. Another church may work in a fall and spring model with summers off. These types of cycles allow for breaks during those seasons when the group participation is likely to wane. It also allows groups to regroup on a regular basis, before they get in a rut. When the groups start again, we afford potential participants an easy entry point for jumping on board. At the same time, we offer ourselves a helpful starting line for deploying new group leaders, so that the total number of groups is steadily expanding.

Whenever I work with churches around the idea of developing a system of small groups, someone invariably asks, "Can the choir be my small group?" or "Can the praise band be my small group?" My answer is "Yes, of course, *if* . . . if you all will sit down and share a meal together before or after, if you will work to integrate newer participants weekly, if you will break into groups of six or so to share what's going on in your lives, if you will pray together weekly, and if you will open a Bible for a time of reflection at least once a month." Doing all of that and getting prepared to lead a worship service the following Sunday will require most of an evening. Many music leaders would just rather get down to business and focus on music for ninety minutes and leave the small group experience for another venue. Either approach is fine.

Churches that thrive in their small group life are virtually unanimous in the conclusion that small groups must be seen as the main event in the church's life, often as more essential than the large-group worship service. They also know that there must be a multiplication of group leaders if there is to be a multiplication of groups and group participants.

Healthy groups need a leader, a shepherd, and two apprentices—in other words, one person who convenes meetings or facilitates projects, another person who tends to keeping up with and nurturing group members, and then two persons being mentored, one by the leader, and one by the shepherd.

If you choose community, a major piece of your job as pastor/leader will be to *pray for new group leaders, to recruit new group leaders, and to see to it that they are trained.* This is essentially the core job description for a new church pastor. And it should be the lead item in the job description of any pastor. Jesus spent the vast majority of his time in leadership development with his band of twelve. The old world way of looking at church leadership has you focused on selecting the right people for the church committee structure. If you choose life and community, you will come to see that developing group leaders is far more critical to your mission.

In either aspect of your choosing community, in your choice to more closely link your church's life with the life of the people around it, and in your choice to lead the people in your church toward more authentic life-sharing with one another, you must lead by example and by experience. Choosing community is, finally, a very personal matter. You, as leader, are choosing to live this value, and to model it. It will not ever work for you to delegate something this important to another if you are going to make community connection a part of your church's DNA. As you think both about outreach and about small groups, ask yourself and ask God how you personally might lead in these endeavors. How might you then bring others along to share the joy you discover and the wisdom you acquire as you live out this powerful decision?

3 CHOOSING FUN OVER DRUDGERY

Several years ago, when the church I served opened our second campus (our Community Life Center), we flooded the nearby neighborhoods with postcards and other publicity that asked folks the question, "Are you having fun yet?" That question puzzled some folks. One man told me that he felt it trivialized a church's purpose to make a point out of having fun.

It so happened that our new facility was bordered on each side by other Christian congregations who were, in contrast, a bit morose and overly serious. Neither of these neighboring churches enjoyed reputations as centers of fun and joy. In the first weeks that we were open, hundreds of community persons flooded into our building and into the life of our church at every level. And we worked hard to ensure that they had fun in their time with us! In our culture most people will instinctively choose joy and fun over drudgery every time. To the extent that we can frame what Christianity is about in terms that are hopeful, joyful, and playful, we will rarely have a shortage of people.

You may find it hard to imagine any church consciously choosing drudgery. In fact, we almost always call it something different—discipline, tradition, duty, liturgy—what have you. The fact that we seek to hide dull, monotonous, religious routine behind such words, in fact, diminishes the value of healthy discipline, tradition, duty and liturgy in our lives.

The word *fun* does not appear in most English Bibles, except in one very informal translation. The closest we get to it in most translations is *joy*, a word that appears between 105 and 191 times. Yes, you heard that right. Different translation teams employ the word *joy* more often than others. The Good News Bible is the most joy-filled, with 191 usages of the word *joy*. The Message is on the other extreme, with only 105; but it uses the word *fun* 35 times, which we can add to the 105 and get 140 uses. The Bible is a joyful book. Christianity is an exuberant and happy faith.

I have seen both liberal and conservative churches that take themselves far too seriously, tediously tending to some liturgical, programmatic, or ideological agenda with little regard for whether or not anyone was being blessed. I have also seen a few that went beyond a healthy playfulness to the point that they cheapened the sense of the holy in worship. It is hard to explain how the latter occurs. Because there is nothing inherently wrong with funny or playful things happening at church any more than there is anything inherently wrong with really great music sung in church. Fun elements in the life of a church become counterproductive only when we pursue them as ends in themselves (that is, for entertainment's sake), rather than as a happy path toward something greater (deeper connection with God). And sometimes we confuse sarcasm (veiled anger) with humor, almost always with negative implications in a church's life.

As we think about having fun in the context of faith community, I would like to consider several venues for it: worship, small group settings (committees and otherwise), ministry teams, and then specifically the ministry of evangelism.

THE FUN STARTS IN BIG CHURCH

When I was a kid, I loved it when my mom said I could go with her to *big church*. Big church was where the bigger people were, but it was also in the big room; it was the big event. Worship is almost always the big event, the largest gathering of persons in any one time or place in the life of a church.

When I served as pastor of the Community Life Center in Gulf Breeze, Florida, we were known for playful, contemporary worship—using a minimum of traditional elements, a lot of recent music, and surprises almost weekly. Because of this, we attracted hundreds of new people in just a few months after opening up, with more than half the crowd on any given Sunday having been active in no faith community a year earlier.

The Community Life Center was one campus of a multisite mainline church, the Gulf Breeze United Methodist Church. Great worship happened seven times a Sunday in that church on three sites—with two of the seven services traditional by coastal Florida standards.

Often, much more energy and joy is poured into the new "contemporary" service than into the traditional service. This is one reason why churches that offer a competently led service with contemporary music usually discover it to become their most attended service in only a few years. There is nothing endemic to "contemporary" that makes it more winsome and appealing than "traditional." Most people crave a little of both. In most cases where one type of worship service outgrows the other, there is simply freshness and a sense of creativity about worship (or a quality of music!) at one hour that is not as apparent at the other hour. Also, the average age is typically lower at the service with guitars and drums.

In the years after I left the Community Life Center, most Sundays saw me on the road, working with this church or that. On those Sundays when I was home, sometimes I would attend an Episcopal church in my neighborhood. My local Episcopal church was the exact opposite of the Community Life Center in many of its liturgical instincts. Christ Episcopal Church in Pensacola is a high church kind of place, with a rich tapestry of well-worn worship traditions and rituals woven into the weekly experience. The Community Life Center is decidedly casual, with worshippers in khaki shorts, carrying their Starbucks in from the lobby. But both places are joy-filled places where a good number of persons meaningfully encounter God on any given Sunday! And that's the point.

Recently, I had occasion to visit with the fellow who worked alongside me as worship leader in my years as pastor at the Community Life Center. Jeremy and I had not chatted in several months. In the course of the conversation, I discovered that he and his family were also worshipping with an Episcopal church in the community where they lived. Both the pastor and the worship leader who built one of the largest contemporary worship communities in northwest Florida are equally attracted to quality, joyful *traditional* worship.

The point: It isn't about contemporary versus traditional. It's about joy and positive energy! And it is about what will work best to reach the community, not about what will enhance my own fine sense of good taste. It should be *fun* to go to worship, regardless of the particular liturgical style.

The following can bring a sense of fun to any worship service in any liturgical tradition:

- Gentle humor shared by the preacher
- Music that the average person can hum on the way home
- Color and festive décor in the room
- A mix of predictability and surprise in the order of elements
- A guest music artist whose music is going to be a WOW for most of those in attendance that day
- An interview, where two people briefly interact off-script, talking about their lives, a recent mission project, or other relevant experience
- Taking worship outdoors once or twice a year when the weather is most likely to cooperate. (Even bringing pets on those Sundays!)
- The experience of "aha!", of God talking to me, discovering an insight into my life, directly rooted to the Scriptural text
- Pleasant, appropriate interaction with other people before, during, or after the worship service, where I am led to feel valued and important, without embarrassment or awkwardness
- A special event outside the worship service itself—something going on in tandem with the indoor experience that engages my interest and increases the sense of energy on campus. Examples include a music ensem-

ble between services in the church courtyard, a hot air balloon ride on Ascension Sunday, really good refreshments above and beyond the usual fare, fifty flamingos in the yard to celebrate the choir director's fiftieth birthday, a giant jigsaw puzzle that is in fact a group photo of the church taken a few weeks earlier, popcorn and a silent black-and-white movie of a recent church event, a Habitat team building a storage shed between 9 in the morning and noon in the church front yard to auction off as a part of a promotion to invite others to invest in Habitat for Humanity, the youth preparing dinner for the senior adults, any playful ministry exhibit highlighting opportunities for participation and volunteering, a small petting zoo *with sheep* on the Sunday when the text is "All like sheep have gone astray," . . . and the list could go on.

If you are concerned about diminishing the reverent atmosphere in the worship room, consider what can be done elsewhere on campus to generate energy and playfulness.

FUN IN SMALL GROUP SETTINGS

There should always be a pot of coffee, freshly brewed, for any small group setting, be it a study group or a ministry team. I recall the night I was driving to lead a visioning event at a church in Coffeeville, Alabama. I was dreaming of a good cup of coffee for the last hour of that journey—only to discover that the church did not even own a working coffee pot. A coffee pot is a ten-dollar investment toward creating a more hospitable environment for your church. Every gathering of church life needs simple refreshments, starting with coffee. When the refreshments become too complicated, the fun can become drudgery, and that is what we are trying to avoid. Occasional homemade goodies are wonderful, but simple refreshments are adequate—and necessary. Serve refreshments on the front end, not at the conclusion when people are rushing to leave.

Take five minutes to do intentional community building before plowing into any tedious meeting agenda. Community building can be sharing prayer requests, sharing the happiest thing that has happened to us today, or arranging ourselves in the order of our birthdays around the room, and then sharing with our newfound neighbors about our all-time favorite birthday present. Such activities should be well-planned to happen quickly and effectively without wasting valuable group time. But they can warm up a gathering immensely and help engender relationships between group members. And always work to the margin—the group leader(s) should intentionally relate to the newest or least active persons in the room.

Stop at one hour when at all possible, or at ninety minutes if you are combining two of the following elements: study, mission, fellowship, or decision making. Meetings of more than ninety minutes should not be the norm, although longer meetings are needed occasionally, for purposes of planning, careful consideration of an issue, or completion of a mission-related task. When the meeting is designed to exceed ninety minutes, I recommend rotating the meeting venue. Long meetings are more effective in fresh settings.

Keep the gathering upbeat and positive. Whether you are doing Bible study or trying to solve a ministry problem, set the ground rules up front. We aren't here to wring our hands, but to have fun searching and discovering, with God and one another. If a group member gets on a political or theological tangent that inhibits the functioning of the group, take the person aside as soon as possible to ask them to respect the diversity of the group. If the group is coming together to deal with a shortage of money in the life of the church, I highly recommend beginning the meeting with humor and possibly a brief time of worship.

We sometimes try to develop new people spiritually by putting them on church decision-making committees. The last thing most people need in their lives is a committee job. They need community; they need to get beyond themselves and invest in the lives of others; but they do not need to be locked in a room making decisions for endless hours about the institutional church. Anyone who comes to a church in order to get on an administrative committee is someone who probably does not need to be on such a committee. But a few people do have to make decisions for churches—and we had best create a positive environment for such work.

If you are leading a decision-making body, please help the group take positive action on something before you go home. Sometimes, considerable conversation and planning prior to the gathering is necessary in order that the decision making can be possible in a short time frame. Decide something. Groups that make significant decisions are fun to be a part of. Groups that then act to live out their decisions are even more fun. We feel momentum in such settings; we feel like we are part of a God-thing. We feel like we are truly, steadily, changing the world.

There are different styles of group study, but in general the smaller the group, the greater the need that the study be interactive. Interactive does not mean reading a Bible passage and then pooling our ignorance: "What do you think it means? Oh-h-h, and what do *you* think it means?" Interactive simply means involving people in application of the passage to their lives. There is always going to be some subjectivity involved in application. *An effective study group offers both objective teaching and subjective interpretation.* To the degree that we get the balance right, the interaction will be experienced as meaningful, even fun. Too subjective, and it will seem like silly conjecture; too lecturelike, and it will seem authoritarian and also become boring with all but the most charismatic leaders.

When it is time to leave, walk as a group out to the street. If there is "clean up" to do, share it among the group. And leave together if possible. This is good for a variety of reasons, safety included, but chiefly in order to carry the relationships all the way out the door to the parking lot or the sidewalk.

HAVING FUN WITH CHALLENGING TASKS

Three tasks that scare the bejeebers out of many church people are evangelism (however defined), fund raising, and recruiting workers for children's ministry. I will to speak to each task.

First, *evangelism.* The word means *good news,* so it should not engender fear. We are sent into the world bearing incredibly wonderful news. Our apprehension about sharing the Christian good news stems in large part from bad stereotypes of obnoxious people pushing their beliefs on others or visitation teams bothering mild-mannered church visitors in their homes on Tuesday evenings when we would all rather be home with a glass of wine or watching TV. Also, most people feel inadequate when it comes to putting their faith into words that sound good. So, it is very easy to just tell ourselves that *religion is best left a private matter*—a value that will poll strongly among almost any gathering of mainline church people.

I want to open the windows of this building and shout to the streets the way the television anchor did in the movie *Network*, and say, "Lighten up, people!"

Can we not have fun? Can we not be playful? Can we not exercise good manners? Can we not say with our words and deeds simply that we are interested in other people, that we are interested in what they are thinking about life and God? There is nothing to memorize. Can we not agree to just avoid klunky, canned conversations, and, rather, intentionally develop authentic relationships with our neighbors and coworkers . . . so that we know something more about them than that they drive a Camry and have two children that are, we think, both in high school? When we experience a major breakthrough in our own spiritual search or adventure, can we not write a letter to a friend to share what is happening with us? If something is going on at church that we enjoy a lot, can we not invite a friend to come along with us or to help us serve refreshments afterward?

In fact, if there *is* much fun going on at church, newcomers rarely have to be coached to invite someone else to join them. It's only those of us who have developed the habit of going to church alone all these years who have difficulty with this. The more people in the room who are relatively new to church, the more inviting of others will naturally occur.

Occasionally, there will be times when a church needs to distribute door-hangers or do a survey at the mall accompanied by an invitation to a community event. In such moments, let the extraverts lead us! And then let's go en masse, make a party of it, and get the job done in a couple hours.

Next, raising money. Any vibrant church will occasionally face a challenge that has a significant price-tag. Our pastoral staff met with Ken Callahan several years ago, and asked the question, "When should we launch the campaign to raise the five million dollars we need for building expansion?" I expected him to respond, "When you fill the current building to 80 percent capacity twice on Sunday morning," or something like that. But his answer was simply this: "When you are ready to have great fun raising five million dollars. That is when it is time to raise the money."

When the vision and the possibilities so overwhelm us that we can't help but take the next step and draw pictures and share the vision with anyone who will listen, and then invite all who will to give toward making the dream come true—that is when it is time for a capital fund-raising campaign. And if you have been a part of a campaign where the energy and vision caught fire in a congregation, you have to admit, it got to be a lot of fun!

The same principal applies to *recruiting children's ministry leaders* and helpers. Though many churches may seek to just avoid evangelism and intentional fund raising altogether, it is hard to avoid the recruiting of children's workers.

Early on in my ministry, I was put in charge of children's Sunday school in a suburban church. We had nine children's classes, packed full. I saw that in order to grow, each class needed to be divided. That would mean double the numbers of teachers. But to get the teachers, more team-teaching had to happen, so that people were not as likely to say "no" to the invitation. So that meant doubling again the number of teachers. I had one summer to quadruple the number of children's Sunday school teachers in order to help our church expand. I called nearly every one of the eighteen hundred members in the church and found my last teacher somewhere in the W's. The Z's got off easy that time. Though the strategy worked, I have never again called a church directory from A to W by myself. *It just wasn't fun enough to want to do it again.*

The next time I needed to recruit a batch of children's leaders, I grouped the eighteen classes into three broad divisions, then invited the leaders of the divisions to each bring a friend and gather in an office with multiple phone lines, where we worked it like a telethon, celebrating and high-fiving each other every time someone agreed to serve. That was twenty years ago. Today, churches that excel in recruiting large children's ministry teams rarely sequester the children and teachers in small cubicle classrooms anymore. Today, we have storytelling and celebratory music led by special teams in large group settings, and then different teams working for twenty minutes in a learning activity with small groups of children, involving crafts, drama, or other activity that reinforces the day's learning with a lot of fun along the way. *Wherever the teachers have as much fun as the kids, there will always be plenty of adults in the children's ministry area.* But even in a joyful environment, it still takes prayer, tenacity, teamwork, and a lot of fun to recruit all the workers you need.

Whatever it is we do as a church, we must find ways to have fun in the doing! Drudgery is deadly.

4 CHOOSING BOLD OVER MILD

What used to pass for coffee in this culture doesn't quite do the trick anymore. Even McDonalds has traded what many in the 1970s considered the most dependably good cup of coffee in town for this high octane stuff they call *Premium*. Maybe the proliferation of Starbucks has driven this. Or maybe Starbucks and McDonalds have just skillfully read the tea leaves (or coffee beans, in this case) and then marketed in sync with the times. In the early years of the twenty-first century, it is clear to me that *bold* is trumping *mild* hands-down. And it isn't just coffee.

Our mild Anglo-Saxon eating habits in middle America have been accosted by an influx of Mexican and Thai restaurants and a jovial guy named Emeril who preaches on the Cooking Channel the need to "kick it up a notch." Kicking it up a notch is more than simply good advice for gumbo. It extends beyond food.

It has become almost impossible to get elected to high office in the United States trying to straddle political middle ground. To get elected these days, the voters want to see a little mad-dog passion in a candidate's eyes, and a bold, "love me or leave me, but here is where I stand" position on some key issues that reflects one's heart and passion. Welcome to the era of the bold!

Boldness is nothing new. Society is constantly going mild on us in various ways. Bold movements challenge our mildness and our ambivalence—and sometimes correct it.

In the book of Acts, the Holy Spirit rushed like a gale-force wind into the mild-mannered Mediterranean synagogues of the first century, stamping people with a bold new brand of faith. And guess what happened? *Bold* trumped *mild.*

Starting in the 1700s, freedom movements and democratic uprisings began toppling monarchs and empires in a process that culminated in the twentieth century. In one way or another, the mildness and social stability of the old world has been tossed out in almost every country on earth, in favor of risky, messy democracy—one of the boldest and most audacious forms of government ever invented.

Bold most always wins over mild—except where boldness is associated with overbearing, dysfunctional excess. Whenever boldness leads to emotional excess in worship or to xenophobic excess in politics, when *bold* becomes extreme or foolish, then *mild and balanced* may save the day. However, despite the attention given to a few bad politicians and loose cannon preachers, *bold* should not be understood as a synonym for *stupid*. *Bold* simply connotes clarity, courage, creativity, and cutting to the chase.

On most days, we are wise to put our money on *bold*.

WHEN BAPTISTS GO BOLD

For the first twenty-three years of my life, I was Southern Baptist. In the late 1970s, when I was in high school, a group of very conservative men put together a very bold plan to take over the Southern Baptist denomination—and within a decade, they had pulled it off (and run me off)! The insurgent group called themselves the Conservatives and cast the status quo leadership as the Liberals. The status quo group wasn't particularly liberal in the broader stream of American theology, and so they cast this political struggle as between the Fundamentalists and the Moderates. In calling themselves the Moderates, they thought they were reframing the political terrain in their favor. They failed to understand that in the rising Era of the Bold, the last thing most folks wanted to be was Moderate. For a lot of folks in this brave new world, the term Moderate is the worst possible epithet that you could hurl at a person. It reeks of ambivalence, of dispassionate aloofness from life, of timidity, of hesitancy to take a stand. It should be no surprise that the Baptist Fundamentalists routed the Moderates, even though some of their beliefs were decidedly beyond the mainstream consensus of that denomination's population. Whatever it was that the Moderates were seeking to preserve, moderation was a bad way to frame it!

As I have continued to watch the Southern Baptists almost my entire adult life from the safe distance of another denominational family, I have observed that the vast majority of ground-breaking ministry innovations over the last two decades in the Baptist world have not come from the

Moderate-Liberals, but rather from the Fundamentalist-Conservatives.

The latter group hasn't been that conservative at all really. *Liberal* and *conservative* were, in this case, merely abstract labels thrown around in a denominational food fight. The group that won power in the Southern Baptist Convention has transformed the theological conversation, the nature of worship, and the structure of congregations more radically and more rapidly than any previous time in the life of that denominational tradition. The supposed conservatives led the parade in dumping the denominational identification from their church names. If you want to go into a Baptist church in Atlanta that still worships, studies, and meets in ways that feel like 1979, you are not likely to find this in one of the churches that sided with the Fundamentalist-Conservatives. You are more likely to find it in one of the churches that sided with the Moderate-Liberals. So much for the value of labels! It was never about *conservative* and *liberal;* it was about *bold* and *mild*—and *bold* won, big time. Furthermore, as a group, moderate Southern Baptist congregations (and congregations that used to be such before they disaffiliated with the SBC) now have declining statistics that mirror the Presbyterians and the Episcopalians.[11] Not only did they lose the battle on the floor of the Southern Baptist Convention, they are slowly losing it in parish churches back home as well.

One more observation: In 1975, the Moderates, still in control, led the denomination to adopt a plan for world evangelization by the year 2000. They called it "*Bold* Mission

11. In checking around, no one can show me these statistics. But key observers sympathetic to the Moderate side, and to its denominational splinter group, the Cooperative Baptist Fellowship, confirm that most of these churches are in slow decline.

Thrust." Since then, the SBC International Missions Board has held together in its work better than any other large missionary-sending agency of an American denomination. The Baptists didn't evangelize the whole world in the last quarter of the twentieth century, but they did maintain a significant missionary enterprise around the world during a time when most mainline mission agencies were slashing the numbers of missionary appointments and cutting funding. *Boldness* has not hurt the Southern Baptists.

To use a political term laden with some baggage, boldness often *rallies a base* of passionate supporters, even when the boldness is a bit controversial or offensive to some. And no institution (religious, political, or corporate) will survive long in the twenty-first century without a *passionate* core community of support, which reaches into the current young adult population and has a mission far beyond preservation of the status quo. If the goal is to offend no one (which is the goal in many churches), or even worse to offend no one currently attending, the church's passion will usually become directed toward preserving fellowship and harmony among the aging church population. And then, mildly, oh so mildly, the offertory organ music will hum everyone into a happy spiritual coma.

MR. ROGERS–STYLE WORSHIP IS KILLING US

Most of us are familiar with the children's television program from the late twentieth century, *Mr. Rogers' Neighborhood.* Fred Rogers was an extremely mild-mannered Presbyterian minister who had a knack for engaging two-year-olds and annoying the rest of the human population. Many Protestant worship services feel to me like something Fred Rogers could lead. Quiet, calm, plodding, and insufferably boring, these services invite us to stand, sit, and move through the script, while someone monologues us to sleep. About halfway through is story time, followed by refreshments, served to us as we stand and walk down front in a quiet, orderly line. Often these services deal in profound truth, but they do so in ways that simply do not engage the young adult public. And many young men, in particular, would rather spend an hour in hell than watch *Mr. Rogers* or sit in our church pews.

In my experience, the apex of the mildness and boredom is usually not the preaching. It is the offertory. The typical American "offertory" strikes me as the epitome of *mild*. It is a symbol worth our attention, especially since most churches reaching young adults in significant numbers choose to have no instrumental offertory. The meditative organ music that takes up five minutes during the collection of money in thousands of mainline churches is, in my estimation, the most deadening thing happening in those places, even worse than the drone of announcements. It is utterly predictable, utterly tame, safe, and sterile. Ten times worse than elevator Muzak! MILD, MILD, MILD! Why would we expect that *anyone* under the age of fifty (and the majority of folks over fifty) would want to subject themselves to such whining blather? Many times in my consulting work across the nation, I have discovered a whole house full of Christians are being held hostage by the music director or the organist— and not just during the offertory.

The last time I went to Paris, I timed the whole trip around the weekly 5 P.M. Sunday organ concert at Notre Dame. I am among the tiny percentage of Americans who really enjoy *good* organ music, concert quality performances on world-class instruments. But I am also an evangelist, and when I have to choose between engaging the public with the captivating invitation of Jesus and teaching them to enjoy the music of an arcane instrument, it is an easy call.

The Mr. Rogers test: if any element of our worship service would fit comfortably on *Mr. Rogers' Neighborhood,* we need to think seriously about either not doing that thing any longer or doing it in a bolder, edgier way, so that it sparkles like a diamond.

Boldness in the world of sound means, for starters, pulling the stops out at times—and then plunging into total silence, so we can hear our hearts beat. Mild churches are uncomfortable with either. It means rich variety of sound . . . flute and steel guitar, perhaps not played together . . . but maybe. It means creating music that captivates people and pulls them to their feet wanting to cheer. It means spending as much money as we can afford on a sound system! (We are not competing with the church down the street, but with the Dolby system at the stadium cinema.)

Bold sound *always* must include percussion. If there is one instrument that is basic to virtually all cultures, it is the drum. Drumming cuts to the very DNA of the soul, to the core rhythms of the *imago dei,* the closest thing to the language of the Spirit you will ever get in most mainline churches. It is the most relevant of all instruments, the opposite of the church organ. Have a percussionist play with bold abandon through the collection of money (with no melody at all) and watch what happens to the energy in the room. Or invite a steel drum band if there is one in your area. Just watch! And then with the drumming continuing, finally add a line of melody from one of their favorite worship songs, and your people will sing their hearts out. If you have ever seen any of the Cirque de Soleil shows that tour about the land, the magic is partly visual, but profoundly based in the incredible ever-changing percussion. Cirque de Soleil is bold. Every worship team should sit through one of those shows (or Blue Man Group) live and then talk about what happened in the room.

Boldness in the world of sight means a never-ending array of fresh symbols, vivid color, and carefully developed visual metaphors in worship. (If you are going to talk about Abraham and Sarah setting off toward the Wild West, bring a covered wagon in and set it down front in full regalia. During the children's sermon, if you do one of those, let the kids get inside the wagon. There may be a local museum that would work with you either to share such a thing or to help you build a simple replica.) Visual boldness may mean taking the gold plated cross off the wall and raising a rough-hewn wooden cross in the middle of the nave and flooding it with light in an otherwise darkened room. Visual boldness could mean a slide show of evocative photos intermixed with paintings of Jesus from multiple cultures, choreographed to Aretha Franklin's version of "Bridge over Troubled Water." This kind of thing engages people of diverse ages and tastes.

If no one on the worship planning team demonstrates this kind of creativity, enlarge the team! Add someone who is new to the faith; add a couple folks who are part of the prevailing demographic that the church is seeking to reach. Get some folks in the room who will become energized around the challenges of throwing together bold offerings of sound and image into your worship experience. There are a lot of folks who spend more time in October planning their Halloween party than they do on their day job. Offer an outlet for such creative energy—find a few of these party people and let them do their magic!

Now, I should say here: current evidence suggests that the rising generation of young adults has little expectation of weekly sound and light shows in worship. This is a generation that tends to value integrity and authenticity over showiness and big productions. But they *do* attend concerts and movies. And we all love a great party. An occasional sound and light show may move people and engage them in profound ways. Grand experiments in worship do not need to be a weekly occurrence, but every six or eight weeks, go for it! Catch them by total surprise!

GIVE THEM JESUS AND THE SPIRIT

Ultimately, the boldness of the Christian faith is contained in the message itself. The gospels are filled with radical teachings that mild-mannered pastors are always trying to sugar coat or downplay in order not to offend middle America. The good news is that in the Era of the Bold, there is no longer any reason to serve as a spin-doctor for Jesus. Just let him say what he says, and let the chips fall where they may. People want that! They are tired of spin and equivocation. They want bold.

In case you haven't noticed—*bold* doesn't get bolder than Jesus. Preach the stuff that Jesus taught, and you can turn off the Power Point machine if you wish. The message itself is so bold, so spiritually ingenious that it will engage people like nothing else on the planet. Let them feel the tension and the ragged edge of his message, and even teenagers will study verse by verse with you, forgetting time and place. Don't soft peddle Jesus. Make his life and teaching front and center for whatever your church does. If a few folks are uncomfortable with the material, let them work out their discomfort directly with God—don't feel a need to release them from that tension.

Beyond Jesus, there is the experience of the Living Spirit of God—the Presence that gets in the room with us, and that gets in our brain with us, the Pentecost factor. When the Spirit of God fell upon the apostles in Jerusalem, we are told they were filled with boldness. In the last hundred years, we have seen a worldwide resurgence of appreciation for the reality of the Holy Spirit. The Pentecostal movement that has swept Latin America as well as large parts of the Third World is an example. Even in the more established bastions of institutional Christianity, churches that boldly celebrate the gifts and surprises of the Holy Spirit are growing, while milder forms of church are fading away. Even if you do not emphasize the gift of tongues or believe in second blessings, I encourage you to let a few Pentecostal Christians liven up your church! I cannot imagine my work as a pastor being nearly as effective without the practices that Pentecostal Christians have taught me along the way.

The sacrament (and I consider it a sacrament) of prayers for healing and this new thing we call "prayer walking" about town—these are gifts to us from the Pentecostal edge! Accept these gifts with thankfulness and play with them. If you do not already do so, offer intentional moments and places where the people of God can anoint the sick with oil, lay hands on them and calmly, boldly pray for their healing. Get a group of folks and regularly walk about town, and lay hands on elementary schools and bus stops and honky-tonk bars. Pray for the people who come to those places. Ask God to speak to you, to show you what you need to see as you walk. Then afterwards, meet to compare notes back in the Fellowship Hall.

Teach your people the concept of spiritual gifts. Work to help folks think theologically about their gifts and talents, and then to think practically about how best to deploy these skills for the glory of God, in light of the needs and opportunities God has shown them.

BOLD INCURSIONS INTO THE SECULAR CITY

In the Book of Acts, the boldness that came from the Spirit was mission driven. It propelled the young Christians into the streets. It propelled the first apostles to other cities, taking the Christian good news to synagogues and halls of power throughout the Roman world. It is not clear whether Paul finally got a live hearing before the Caesar, but in time, the whole empire was transformed by the growing impact of Christianity. (Granted, the Romanization of Christianity warped it—the price of success for any spiritual movement is holding on to its soul once the people in power buy in, and they then come to treat their new religion like they would a new acquisition of property, something that is *theirs* to use and modify according to their needs and agenda.)

The nature of the mission is somewhat changed from the first century context, and also never-changing. At one level the church exists to help individuals discover and apply Christ's good news to their lives and needs, in all eras. Furthermore, the church exists to grow people as servants of that good news on a variety of fronts, both in word and in deed. Finally, together we want to change the world for the better, and the best strategies for doing this are constantly evolving. We want to shake the foundations of social systems in order to make the world a fairer, kinder place where all people can enjoy their share of life's blessings and hopes. The end sounds mild enough, but getting there requires us to boldly confront the powers and power brokers of the current world order.

The bolder a church's vision is with regard to the preceding, the more engaging and winsome that church becomes to the general public. The milder the vision expressed, the more that energy is diverted to fellowship, childcare, and building renovation, to entertainment activities, parties, and trips. The mild church is a religious Elk's Lodge except for about an hour a week, when we sit quietly in a room decorated to my grandmother's tastes and try to think (and even sing) nice thoughts about Jesus and loving others, as our leaders run around down front in sixteenth-century costumes. Indeed there is a place in the world (and a market) for fraternal organizations such as the Elks. But the Elks total membership is headed the same direction as the Episcopalians.

But the bold church is quite serious in its intent to change the world, within its range of influence, empowered by God. In a busy world of working, commuting, child-rearing, and grocery shopping, I will give some time to a movement that promises to help me find wise solutions for my life and to truly improve my community and world. I, personally, do not have much time for the Elk's Lodge *or* much time for a church whose primary purpose is camaraderie. And I stand with a majority of young Americans on this point. If I do belong to an organization with mild aspirations, I will be casual and sporadic in my attendance, volunteering, and giving. My energy will drift elsewhere.

Some churches have adopted sister villages, churches, and other faith communities in the Sudan and in other places of tremendous need. Such churches thrive more often than not. They have declared that they desire to bring to pass the reign of God more fully in some of the toughest corners of the earth. That's a bold thing to attempt. The boldness of such vision activates people. I lost count of the people who came into Gulf Breeze Church because they first went along with us on one of our mission trips to relieve human suffering, or the people who got involved with us on a project to improve life in our own community. Bold visions for changing the world will always win us partners who are ready to roll up their sleeves, and in such endeavors they and we together open up ourselves to the serendipitous discoveries and life changes that happen when we are sharing life with the poor and giving to make life better for others.

Rock my world in worship. Introduce me to the unabridged Jesus and to the experience of the Holy Spirit in her wildness. Challenge me to join with you in changing the world. Be bold and you will win my undivided attention.

5   CHOOSING FRONTIER OVER FORTRESS

I once consulted with a white Episcopal priest whose church met in an African American neighborhood of an East Coast city. He was trying hard to immerse himself in neighborhood life, and to network with folks who might, together, be keys to a new beginning for his church. But there remained one big problem (in addition to the church folks themselves, who were not much into mixing with the neighborhood folks). The problem was that their church building looked like a castle. It was nothing short of *scary* for most of the people who walked by it. It was like Fort Apache, screaming to the passersby, "Don't even think about scaling these walls!"

A lot of churches with friendlier buildings still surround their gathering place on Sunday morning with a line of high-end automobiles, broadcasting silently and clearly to all who would dare enter that "This place belongs to rich people. You are welcome to come in, sit down, and worship here, but don't forget who owns this place." You may counter that there is no one in your current church membership who feels such a thing. I have difficulty believing that your church is entirely free of elitist attitudes, but I would reply, "If you are serious about including neighbors who cannot afford a "Beemer"—park down the street, better yet, leave it at home. And dress down a little bit for Sunday services." But only if you are serious about creating a hospitable environment for people of all economic classes!

Most churches become fortresses. This is especially true of churches in urban areas where the majority of members now commute from the suburbs. This is a tricky topic because there may not be a conscious fortress mentality among the church membership. Nonetheless, there may be a fortress *perception* within the community. In many urban settings, despite the best of intentions it is extremely hard to avoid at least some degree of fortress perception.

THE FORTRESS TEST

Respond to each of the statements below with *true* or *false*.

- Less than six persons a year join our church from *within a mile* of our church building (or within our building's zip code).

- *All* doors to our church building(s) are locked during weekdays, even if some have an intercom and buzzer.

- The major outside doors from the street to our church's *worship space* have no windows to see inside.

- There are *warning signs* posted on our church property for *any* of the following: skateboarders, loiterers, unauthorized parking, trespassing on the playground, bringing firearms in the building, etc.

- There is an imposing tower or steeple *attached to* our church building.

- Our facilities are closed for business (other than the church office) most of the time during weekdays.

- The cars in the parking lot or on the street around our church buildings typically are far more expensive than the cars you see in our neighborhood.

- Ninety percent of church group gatherings and ministries are held inside our buildings (as opposed to elsewhere in the community).

- There are no flowers blooming near the main entrance to the worship space. (Or no fountain running—fountains are as good as flowers. If you have a fountain, we will let you off the hook for the lack of flowers!)

- The church phone number sends me to an answering machine during daytime hours.

- None of our weekly worship services specialize in a style of music that many neighborhood people under the age of fifty would listen to on the radio.

- We pin tags or ribbons on new worshippers labeling them as VISITORS, reminding them that *they are not us.*

- We wait *more than six days* to follow up personally (phone call, custom e-mail, or home doorstep visit) with new worshippers who leave us contact information. (Form letters on church letterhead do not count.)

- We currently lack a weekday ministry for neighborhood children of any sort (preschool, after school, tuition based or free) at least one day a week.

- The official church sign on the street either offers no specific invitation to a specific event or invites me only to worship services.

Most mainline churches will answer *true* to more than half these questions. To those churches, I say, "Just imagine what could be if you took action on several of the items where you have the leverage to make changes!"

Some churches, of course, have no building at all. They are most often new churches or churches in the process of relocation, where one facility has been sold and another is being constructed. They may rent or borrow a facility. When a church lacks a building or moves out of a building during a season of renovation, good things often happen in their life. Even long-time members may note that things feel less stuffy, more down-to-earth, that the congregational singing is better in the school cafeteria down the street. This observation is a signal that the church's former building was not working well. If the renovations are simply new paint, carpet, and a few extra ranks to the organ, the church will likely lose the new-found sparkle within a few weeks of moving back into their sacred space. If a church (old or new) moves from temporary space into a really well-designed space, and enters that new space with quality worship and a couple of other signature ministries firing on all cylinders, it is common that such a church will surge forward to new heights of attendance within weeks of entering their new home.

BUILDINGS ARE LIABILITIES

Tom Bandy believes that church buildings should be counted on a spreadsheet as liabilities rather than assets. In many cases, they are necessary liabilities, but I think Bandy has a good point here.

If a church's spreadsheet is merely financial, the church building will usually be perceived as the greatest asset due to the value of real estate in the area. But I am working right now with several churches of under one hundred in attendance, trying to operate in multimillion-dollar facilities where the mounting *necessary* repairs (wiring, roofing, air conditioning) greatly outstrip the churches' financial abilities. Yes, the building is worth a fortune on paper, but it is also an albatross around the church's neck, vacuuming up a disproportionate share of the church's resources and attention away from the real mission.

If the church has an endowment to maintain the building or has sold "air rights," this liability becomes even more insidious. Without large cash reserves, the church may look at the overhead of maintaining the building, decide to sell their property, and relocate to a more sensible center for their ministry. But with an infusion of cash, a church will rarely ever move from a historic property, even long after the buildings have become so obsolete for the current task of community evangelization as to be rendered virtually useless. When financial survival of an institution is assured, the actual numbers of participants becomes less important, in some cases irrelevant to the church's decision making. It should be no wonder that churches in historic facilities rarely grow in the United States. There are wonderful exceptions of bold, brassy ministries being offered from historic sites. But most urban churches in old buildings are either dying or already departed from the earth. If they are not dying, they are typically serving only a fraction of the number of people their buildings were erected to serve. The building may be worth untold millions to some condo developer, but it is often impeding the church's effectiveness in mission. Anything that impedes mission is a liability.

WHAT IF MY CHURCH IS A MUSEUM?

When the bronze historical marker goes on the building, the chances of a church ever escaping that building are greatly reduced. When a church building is more notable for its architectural significance than for its practicality as a tool to serve a diverse new population, I would suggest you consider the following options:

If the location is really ideal for the church's work in the next twenty-five years, consider systematically tearing down everything but the most hallowed historic building, and build a ministry center that makes sense. It will often be cheaper to rebuild from scratch (and to maintain the new construction) than to renovate existing space and keep patching an antiquated structure. Plus, when you start with a blank page, you will not be bound by the old locations of plumbing lines and load-bearing walls. In the cities, many churches will wisely choose to rebuild a high-rise of ten or more stories, where the upper floors can be rented to commercial and residential tenants, helping to fund the community ministries that are housed on the lower floors.

If you are limited by parking issues, neighborhood safety issues, or any number of building issues in an old location, consider selling off part of the land, so that a developer can tear down all but the most hallowed historic building—which you can retain. Take the money and build a second campus somewhere that makes sense. You can retain the historic sanctuary for weddings and special events. You could even continue to hold one Sunday service down there. Occasionally, you might be able to sell to someone who wishes to build a parking garage—or a building with underground parking— parking that can be free to church use on Sundays.

Consider *giving* your historic space to a library association, to another church, to an ecumenical ministry, to a hotel, or to the city—to some group that will take good care of it—and then let them spend the millions to preserve it. This frees you to pick up and relocate your church's ministry, without the guilt that you are somehow offending the god of architectural preservation.

Share space with another ministry or group that will help reduce your church's share of the costs for keeping and running an oversized, antiquated building. Or sell to them and lease back from them. In the expensive real estate market of twenty-first-century urban America, sharing space with old churches is becoming one of the most common strategies for housing the ministries of new and growing churches. There may be a new or growing church within your denominational family that could share your church's facility. Or it may be a church that is of another denomination or of no denomination. In order to achieve a sizeable sharing of financial overhead, you will need to offer the partner church or building occupant a sizable shared *voice* in deciding questions of building maintenance, renovation, and space utilization. If they perceive themselves simply as tenants, their investment in the facility will be minimal. *As you share control, you are more likely to truly share the costs. And vice versa.*

If you are unable to sell, rebuild, or downsize your building liability in an old place, you could simply move significant ministries out of your church building into other spaces. Or start a new thing in a new place! If you can't afford the million dollars needed to make the old fortress an accessible space, take a small portion of the million and invest in the birthing of a new worship community in another space, off campus.

Rent, borrow, buy—whatever you do beats just sitting around waiting to die in the old location.

BACK IN THE GOOD OLE DAYS

In the United Methodist tradition, the good ole days of frontier ministry are no longer within the actual memory of any living human being. In that denomination and within many mainline communities, there are occasional churches that have recreated a frontier approach to ministry that blesses their respective communities. But the last time we saw a widespread frontier mentality among any of the old denominational tribes was so long ago that we rely now upon history books to describe it and to understand it.

From 1790 to 1830, the congregations of the movements who later would become United Methodist typically gathered in space that we would consider unacceptable by current standards. Yet these churches grew from roughly 58,000 adherents in 1790 to about 501,000 in 1830, a growth of nearly 900 percent in forty years.[12] They outpaced population growth three times over, growing from 1.5 to 5.1 percent of the U.S. population during these four decades. In fact, in countless communities across North America, the Methodist Episcopal Church predated the formal founding of the town proper. The movement was so nimble that the churches were organizing faster than the municipalities, essentially arriving prior to the people in some cases! It is estimated that one third of the Methodist Episcopal congregations in 1830 had no building. They met wherever they could, many in homes, some in schoolhouses. Of those churches that had buildings, many had simple clap-

---

12. These and other statistics in this chapter about the diminishing growth and subsequent decline of the United Methodist Church are provided by the General Commission on Archives and History of the UMC (www.gcah.org).

board chapels that would last only a few years before fire or the church's growth would force their replacement.

By the 1840s the movement's growth rate was markedly slowing, about the time American churches began building more substantial buildings. The correlation between the steady slow-down of the Methodist movement's expansion over the next century and the steady construction of larger and more substantial buildings is nothing short of remarkable. I cannot go so far as to declare causality and say that big buildings cause churches to slow down, but I can definitely tell you there is a correlation: the more building-oriented any church becomes, the more it will be tempted to take on the settled attitudes and habits of an institution, and to leave the free-spirited, frontier-oriented attitudes and practices that grew it to start with.

By contrast, from 1960 to 2000, the successor denominations of the Methodist Church collectively lost 21 percent of their people, a net loss of some two million souls. This is what took the denomination's market share down by almost half during these forty years, from 5.9 percent of the population, down to 3 percent. What was, 170 years earlier, one of the most nimble, innovative, and proactive Christian movements in history has become an ossified, aging organization largely incapable of any effective ministry to large swaths of the American population, an overorganized institution struggling to produce just a handful of new churches annually. But where once they worshipped in shacks, the United Methodists now own cathedral-like space, alongside posh parlors and state-of-the-art administrative space in thousands of places. A lot of good all those fortresses accomplished!

It is a story that most denominations could tell—the shift from *frontier* mentality and practice to *fortress* mentality and practice. And though there is an obvious parallel between constructing of physical fortresses and becoming a virtual fortress, it would be inaccurate to treat the fortress mentality simply as an issue of our relationship to real estate. It really does go deeper.

IT'S ALL ABOUT THE MISSION

If asked "What business are we in?" an early Methodist would have shot back a fast answer to that question. They believed their mission was to "reform the nation and spread scriptural holiness over the land."[13] Folks, this is a *bold* mission, if ever I heard one, based in passion for *community*. But this mission is also totally *frontier* in its orientation. It is a mission that pushes the church beyond facilities, which in eighteenth century England had begun to function as fortresses of intimidation toward the working classes.

What business are we in, really? I ask that question in many of the places where my consulting work takes me. The answers I most often hear are "glorifying God," "loving our neighbors," and "winning souls to Christ." It is hard to take a serious crack at the latter two without getting outside the church building. But the same is true even of the first answer, "glorifying God," if we consider that Christianity is as much about making things right in the world as it is about withdrawing into a holy space. So, it is fair to say that almost every answer that I get to the preceding question is a good answer, and an answer that demands a frontier mentality to our church's life.

13. This phrasing of the church's mission comes from John Wesley, presiding over the first Methodist Annual Conference in England in 1744. In terms of reforming, he actually said, "to reform the nation, especially the Church, and to spread . . ."

But when the conversation shifts from ideals to reality, from stated mission to daily life lived in the faith community, our practices are not typically driven by our mission. We exert token efforts in terms of glorifying, loving, and evangelizing. The unstated mission that truly drives most churches is providing fellowship, comforting ritual, and care for insiders. When the conversation begins to call for shifting resources of time and finances toward outreach ministry, I will often hear someone mumbling, "We don't need to work to add more people until we can adequately take care of the ones we have." This statement, which cuts to the heart of the mainline church's dilemma, arises from the belief that the mission of the church is taking care of our own. I wish I could have been in the room the first time a Methodist church member verbalized such sentiment. I would love to have seen the looks of shock on the faces of the others in the room. Such an idea may have been conceivable among occasional Lutherans and Congregationalists back then, but it would have been received as an utterly ridiculous statement in a Methodist meeting, something not seriously to be considered. They understood their mission to be about changing the world, not exhausting all their energy on one another. Yet with their pioneering work in small group life, the early Methodists also exceeded most mainline churches today in the quality of TLC delivered to each church member.

Paul Borden is the architect of one of the most remarkable turnaround projects ever documented in the life of a regional judicatory of a mainline American denomination. Paul shares a bit of that story in the final chapter of this book. Some time back, Paul was teaching a group of leaders in Alabama, and someone posed to him a question about the value of local church mission statements. Paul shrugged. In his experience, he hadn't seen that much difference between the churches who had them and those who did not. But then he added that if a church has one, the key is that it be outward in its focus. I could not agree more! A mission statement needs to point a church out the doors to the frontier, even to the ends of the earth. The mission of God in Christ is about carrying good news to the frontier, not guarding it in the fortress.

To this end, a church that seeks to reclaim its frontier spirit and to move beyond the limitations of its building/ fortress as a primary ministry venue may wish to consider the following possibilities:

Consider partnering with a community center, a YMCA, or a private school to offer an off-site children's ministry event, either a special one-time thing, a short-term thing (like a Vacation Bible School or a day camp), or a weekly thing.

Adopt a school, a hospital, a nursing home, a police station, a fire station, a senior center. In the case of a school or a hospital, if it is too large, adopt a particular unit or a grade level. And then shower the folks in that place with love all year long. You will bless many and come away with more joy even than you give away. (Hey, if you wish to be bold, decide that no child shall leave third grade at the school across the street who cannot read, and then shower that school with reading tutors until you get the job done!)

Instead of doing another tired Christmas cantata in your building, work with a shopping center or other management group overseeing a major public venue and design a Christmas music event that helps them create the festivity they are looking for while introducing your church to hundreds (or thousands) of new friends.

Begin *prayer walking* certain focal neighborhoods in your community with groups of persons from your church on a regular basis. Begin and end at a set location, fanning out in all directions, in teams of two, three, or four. Invite people to just watch for what God wishes to show them, to look for clues of God's presence in the community, and for opportunities to extend and amplify that presence. Always meet back together somewhere for coffee and reflection at the end. After a few weeks, invite people to form into ministry teams to do something together in response to what God is showing them, possibly something in partnership with people they have met in their prayerful wandering. Such ministries will range from home repair to children's sidewalk Sunday school to political advocacy for and with disenfranchised populations.

Start your *next* worship service in a very public and high-traffic place—most mainline churches need to worship in at least two musical/liturgical genres, regardless of size. At Gulf Breeze Church, the last service I helped to start was in an open-air beach bar at 8:30 on Sunday mornings, in a setting where just hours earlier, drunken people had partied the night away, occasionally with wet bikini contests and the like. The service quickly grew to about 150 people on a typical Sunday. At 7 A.M. each week now, the Worship at the Water trailer pulls up with sound system and band equipment, and a rather profane corner of the planet becomes sacred for a couple hours. Every so often one of the partiers collapses at 3 A.M. on the beach and then wakes up a few hours later . . . in church.

Offer a three-week miniseries, an upbeat study with biblical wisdom applied to some practical matter in life, such as navigating life transitions, managing money, strengthening family relationships, or developing a customized life purpose. Plan to teach the series with a team that includes a pastor and at least one specialist in some science related to the series topic, so that you have an intelligent, theological conversation about a practical life concern. But tell your church it can only be taught off-campus. Invite your people to host the study at their place of work or school once a week for three weeks in a conference room during lunch hour. Let them sign up to bring the study to their work place. Make some new friends all over town!

You get the idea. Think frontier!

6   CHOOSING NOW RATHER THAN LATER

Of course there are times when waiting is a good thing. George Washington in the fall of 1775 wanted to attack the British forces that held Boston, and had he done so, the Americans would have been routed. The Continental Congress told Washington to wait a bit. And yet, in the long run, Washington's propensity to act was more of a help than a liability. Finally, Washington's audacity and assertiveness surprised his adversaries and enabled him to frame key battles on his terms.[14] He wasn't one to wait any longer than absolutely necessary.

Even the Continental Congress knew that waiting was a short-term strategy for their army—not a passive strategy but a time for intensive preparation and reinforcement. When it comes to truly urgent matters, you can't wait five years. It may

14. David McCullough, *1776* (New York: Simon and Schuster, 2005).

be hard to wait even five months, although sometimes a short wait can offer a very beneficial prep time. In these cases, we really aren't waiting at all, we are just starting at the beginning, rather than rushing headlong into the middle of the project. For those of you offended by military analogies, my apologies. I committed myself to a life of nonviolence long ago, but I still love Sun-tzu's book *The Art of War*, which teaches me about strategy in high stakes endeavors where at least some of the people out there do not want you to succeed and may stop at nothing to try to block you. Sun-tzu makes the case for being proactive:

> In general, whoever occupies the battlefield first and awaits the enemy will be at ease; whoever occupies the battlefield afterward and must race to the conflict will be fatigued.[15]

On a very different type of battlefield, committed firmly to nonviolence but battling nonetheless, Martin Luther King Jr. wrote an epistle from the Birmingham, Alabama, city jail that will be read for the rest of time. In that letter he writes about time and urgency:

> Actually time is neutral. It can be used either destructively or constructively. I am coming to feel that the people of ill-will have used time much more effectively than the people of good will. . . . We must come to see that human progress never rolls in on wheels of inevitability. It comes through the tireless efforts and persistent work of men willing to be co-workers with

15. Sun-tzu, *The Art of War*, trans. Ralph D. Sawyer (New York: Barnes and Noble Books, 1994), 191.

God, and without this hard work time itself becomes an ally of the forces of social stagnation. We must use time creatively, and forever realize that the time is always ripe to do right. Now is the time to make real the promise of democracy, and transform our pending national elegy into a creative psalm of brotherhood. Now is the time to lift our national policy from the quicksand of racial injustice to the solid rock of human dignity.[16]

If we are about God's work, time is always a precious commodity. Both the prophet Isaiah and the Apostle Paul say to us that "now is the time of salvation." (2 Cor. 6:2) If we understand the work of our church to be less urgent than what the Freedom Fighters were about in the 1960s, perhaps we do not clearly understand the salvation we have been called to offer. There are people all around us who have been living in isolation from God and their neighbors most of their lives. How long do we intend to wait before offering them ministries and relationships through our churches that can help them to reclaim their best selves, to discover the joy of Jesus' way, and to fall more deeply in love with the God who loves them? There are injustices and legacies of human suffering that have endured for all of recorded history. These things utterly dishonor God and humanity—and some of them can be significantly changed in our lifetime. How long do we intend to wait before joining with other persons of good will to do something about economic injustice or gender discrimination or to raise awareness about an unfolding genocide in the world that threatens to annihilate a million people ? Five years? Fifty years? A thousand?

16. Martin Luther King Jr., *Letter from the Birmingham Jail*, 1963.

Or are we intent upon being good stewards of the time God gives us and our generation?

When people get caught up in great salvation movements of God, they tend to choose *now* over *later*. They come to feel a holy urgency about their work. We may learn to deal with the fact that we need considerable time to journey the road from Point A to Point B, but when we are filled with God's urgency, we become passionate about getting on down that road where God is leading us.

REASONS WE PROCRASTINATE

Churches, like human beings, can choose to excel in procrastination. We know we need to do something, but we just aren't of a mind to get started yet. Our reasons for putting off urgent action are as wide-ranging as our capacity for creative thinking, but some of the most common that I hear are as follows:

1. We need to get out of debt first.

2. We need to focus our energy first on a fund-raising campaign or building project—that may have nothing to do with the most urgent matters before us.

3. We need to work first on doing a better job at pastoral care of our current members.

4. We don't have enough workers for the things we are trying to do currently.

5. We need to grow our current ministries to a certain level first before spreading ourselves too thin in something new.

6. We need to help our current pastor make it to her or his retirement first, then hopefully receive a pastor more suited to lead us through the challenge before us.

7. We need to wait until after our new pastor's honeymoon (with the church) is concluded, rather than risk his or her credibility with major change too fast.

8. We want first to spend a couple years on a self-study and discern our mission, vision, and values.

9. We need to wait for Mrs. Smith to die, because she runs the place and she would not like this.

10. There's a new condo development in the mix. When that is built in a couple years, we will have the people we need to do this.

Friends, I have heard them all, at one church or another. And a few of these excuses I hear over and over again. There's enough truth in each statement to intimidate your church into doing nothing. Each statement touches upon a certain wisdom, and then twists it—sort of like the devil did with Jesus in the desert. When people say these things, they are telling me some issues that will need to be explored as they move forward, factored into the roadmap. But more often than not, we use these kinds of issues as excuses to delay action. And then five years later, five years older, fifty people lighter, we feel even more overwhelmed by the challenge than we did earlier.

DEBUNKING THE EXCUSES

If I may speak briefly to each of the excuses in the preceding list, in the same order, perhaps I can help dispel the power of these ideas that are perhaps paralyzing your church:

1. *A little bit of debt will not hurt your church,* especially if the debt is related to the financing of something that is likely to help you grow. The only time I caution a church against

taking on debt is when their attendance is in free-fall, casting question on their future income. If a church is stable, growing, or shrinking very slowly over several decades, usually they can allocate up to 15 percent of their Sunday collection for debt service without disrupting their ministries too significantly. So if that church collects $10,000 in undesignated offerings per month, it could allocate up to about $1,500 in debt service. When churches try to pay down debt more aggressively out of current income, they often starve ministry development. Similarly, when churches are unwilling to take on a little debt, but want to save up over several years to pay cash for a ministry facility that was needed yesterday, they starve ministry development.

2. *Without the ministry initiatives toward new people that are driving a new building, a building itself will yield nothing but an expensive bill for the church.* A lot of churches have "built it" only to discover that "nobody came." A church should focus first on expanding relevant, quality ministry to its area population and learn how to reach new folks without an expensive facility. Then with good momentum established, a new or enlarged facility becomes simply a tool to catch the harvest of people; often such a church will experience a sharp jump in ministry participation when they open such a facility. Focusing first on a funding campaign related to the desired ministry expansion may be a wise thing. However, I observe some of the things mainline churches raise millions to build—a gymnasium for children that we don't have, or a new parlor and bridal suite, or a refurbished and rewired sanctuary—and I know that these new and improved facilities will likely not advance the church's mission at all.

3. *If we wait until we have flawless pastoral care, we are choosing to table new ministry forever.* Thinking that we need

to perfect our care of members before expanding our ministry is as devilish an idea as ever infected a church. Our member care will never be perfect, so this is a perfect rationale for perpetual procrastination of ministries to and for nonmembers.

4. *The lack of workers is a matter for our attention, but not a reason for tabling a ministry advance.* Often the first phase of a ministry advance should be a major leadership development season. Ministry leaders can be drawn from beyond the church membership. Many ministries can be developed in partnership between churches or between churches and other community organizations. Usually when we think of the leader shortage, we keep thinking within the same tiny circle of people who come to our committee meetings. We need to think far beyond this! If we are talking about the building of great leader teams, the cliché "Build it and they will come" is more likely to predict the future.

5. *Thinking that we need to further grow our current ministries before launching something new is tricky.* If our current ministries are growing or can be grown with minor adjustments, then sometimes it will make sense to grow the overall church with the current ministry strategies for a while longer before launching off into the next thing. However, if the ministries are stuck or declining in their attendance, it may be urgent to start something new as soon as possible. The new thing may be the spark needed to get the whole church growing again.

6. *If you are five years from retirement and hesitant to help your church launch something new because you feel tired or incompetent, then you are telling me that, in fact, you are already retired.* You would serve your church well to step into a pastoral situation that demands less proactive leadership. I have watched more than one church help a faithful sixty-some-

thing pastor to the retirement finish line while at the same time nurturing younger staff leadership and innovating boldly in their ministry.

7. *If the turnaround does not begin during the first year of a new pastor's ministry, the chances of it ever coming are diminished.* Occasionally, we see it in year three or year five, but usually it starts in year one. So a new pastor's honeymoon should be seen as a window of opportunity to make a few critical decisions related to the church's future ministry expansion. We don't need wholesale change, redesigning everything at once; we need just a few key changes in strategic areas that send the signal that the future is going to be bright, and a little different.

8. *The children of Israel's forty years in the desert offered the world its first church mission, vision, and values discernment process.* A generation wandered around and died in the wilderness, running from its past and scared of its future. I have led plenty of navel-gazing vision discernment processes in local churches, and observed the same dynamic. What I have learned is this:

- Vision does not descend upon groups. It usually comes to individuals and then is confirmed by the group.

- The churches that have good leaders, solid prayer, and urgency about their mission will gain nothing by a self-study. They will sail to the stars anyway.

- The churches that are paralyzed will gain nothing by a self-study. They will just use the self-study as a stalling tactic.

Rather than take your church through a self-study or visioning process, just start reading the Book of Acts together and prayerfully walking your neighborhood (both your local neighborhood and, through solid educational experiences, your virtual, global neighborhood). God will help you figure out what you need to do.

9. *If we wait for the Mrs. Smiths of the church to die before we make necessary changes, they may outlive the congregation!* These people have an average life expectancy of ninety-eight years, it seems.

10. *If I had a dollar for every time a church told me they were waiting for the loft apartments that were supposed to be coming, I would have a pocket full of cash.* Downtown churches are always holding out hope for the young professionals who are going to come live in the new high-density housing that some developer has planned. Semirural churches are always pointing to the new subdivisions on the horizon. Many of these projects never get built or are more than a decade in materializing. Some churches have actually lived to see the new residences go in, only to discover that the old neighbors (the poor folks in the dilapidated housing) were easier to reach and serve than the young professionals intoxicated with careers and their latest love interests. Serve the population you can find to serve today. Don't bank on tomorrow!

WHY WE CAN'T WAIT

If your church is like most churches, it isn't getting younger.

Most mainline churches, despite occasional financial challenges, have more real dollar income today than they will likely have in the future. It will be harder to afford tomorrow to do what we need to do today.

Do we truly believe that Jesus' invitation "Follow me" can be put off until a more convenient time?

If mainline churches do not become more assertive and begin to grow in number, fundamentalist and non-Christian voices will even further dominate the national (and international) conversation in the years ahead.

Though the number of young adults who distrust organized Christianity is skyrocketing to the highest levels in American history, this is one of the most spiritually minded generations we have seen come down the pike. As Jesus would say, "The fields are ripe for harvesting" (John 4:35). There are millions of nonchurch people talking about the most important things in life, if only we would choose to be a part of their conversation.

WHAT NEXT?

Even if you are committed to act decisively and quickly, you still may be confused as to what exactly to do. Or you may have a good sense, but you want to confirm that with a seasoned leader or a ministry coach/consultant. Some of the best decisions great churches make happen because of either an intensive consultation or an ongoing coaching relationship with someone who sees the big picture and who works with scores of churches. In my last church, we paid several thousand dollars more than once for such help—and it was worth every penny.

There are two approaches to coaching. Your church can contract with someone to work with a range of leaders and staff persons in a churchwide process of assessment and strategic change. Typically *the church will pay* this coach (or coaching team). Or a pastor-leader may wish to contract with someone to coach him or her in appropriate skills and leadership responses to the situation. In the latter case, *the pastor usually pays,* or uses continuing education funds provided by the church. Either strategy can be helpful. If the church's administrative body will embrace the coaching process, growth and positive change will usually come more easily than if the pastor works unilaterally with the coach. You can, of course, do both: bring in someone to work with the whole system and then invite that person (or another) to develop an ongoing mentoring relationship with the pastor for at least another year. To use the metaphor of psychological therapy, there is a significant difference between getting a whole family system in the room together and just sending one family member to counseling. Getting everyone in the conversation is certainly messier at first, but it usually yields more satisfying results for the family. Nonetheless, there are some issues that are just best addressed one-on-one.

Find someone whose work you trust. Find someone who has a track record of positive experience and growth in local churches. Call the pastors of some of those churches, and find out not just whether or not the church liked the consultant, but find out what happened in the wake of the process.

Set up a conference call with the potential coach on the phone, with at least three people on your end of the line. Let the potential coach hear your situation and describe a potential process for addressing that situation. Is the coach responding to you with a preprogrammed agenda or really listening to the uniqueness of your situation? Listen to your gut. It is very important that this person understand and click with your church's culture *to some degree*. Interview more than one such person.

If you are not ready to explore a relationship with a ministry coach, another next step would be to convene a group of leaders from within your church and distribute copies of this book to each. If you like, invite a couple of nonmembers to read along with you, persons whose wisdom you would love to have in the mix. Get together regularly over six weeks and discuss each chapter in light of your church's issues and challenges. This book is not a road map with a list of magical one-two-three's. But it is designed to provoke a helpful conversation. There is no telling where your conversation might go, but *you will certainly be talking about some of the right things,* possibly issues that have not been discussed before at your church or issues that have been previously framed in a way that felt threatening but now may feel less so.

If getting together over six weeks is difficult with people's crazy schedules, ask everyone to read the book in full; then meet for a twenty-four-hour retreat in a lodge somewhere to process the chapters together.

Whatever you choose to do with the thoughts and "aha's!" that may be bubbling up in you, I plead with you simply: do something, and do something soon. Choose *now* over *later!*

THE INVITATION

In segments of the African American church tradition and the southern evangelical tradition, there remains a liturgical component long abandoned in other churches. It is the invitation, the moment in a worship service when people are called to act decisively, based upon their faith in God. In many Euro-American churches the invitation is a call to receive the sacrament. I am, however, talking here of a different invitation, something bolder and gutsier than merely walking down for Holy Communion. I am talking about an invitation to let go of your labored and ineffective efforts to run your own life apart from God, and to turn to accept and begin to walk in the Way of Jesus.

A few years ago I visited the worship service of St. John's United Methodist Church in downtown Houston for the first time. St. John's is a church that meets in a historic building located literally underneath a freeway overpass. I had heard of this unusual urban church that was reaching and serving the central city population of Houston in a remarkable way, growing from twelve to seven thousand congregants in a decade's time. I had heard about their social services center that served the homeless population, their teams that visited inmates in the county jail, and their break-dancing music leader. I had heard about Pastor Rudy Rasmus who wore a baseball cap as he preached in a stained-glass sanctuary. I was most intrigued by the legend that Rudy had never given an invitation at the close of any service in the previous ten years without somebody walking down the aisle to join St. John's Church and publicly self-identify as a follower of Jesus. I enjoyed everything about the service that day, from the liturgical dancers to the gospel choir to the collection of the offering to the waiting line to get in (waiting alongside a fellow first-timer who had, in fact, just gotten out of jail the week before). It was a fun ninety minutes in God's house! But I had come specifically to see Rudy's invitation. I was not disappointed.

At first he gave a rather low-key straightforward invitation to Christian discipleship not unlike what you might hear in many Anglo churches. We sang four verses of the hymn, and one woman wandered down to the front of the room on the last verse. I thought to myself, "The record will hold for another week. Again, at least one person has stepped out to join this church this morning." I did not realize that Rudy was just warming up. After we sang the hymn, he asked us to raise our hands if we were members of St. John's, and then to share with our neighbor why it was that we had decided to join this church. So all across the room, people quietly began visiting with one another, sharing faith stories about how they came to this church. Then he asked those who were new or who had not yet made such a commitment to share with their neighbor how long they had been attending, and if they were not members, to share what held them back. Again, a murmuring of conversation filled the sanctuary. Then he instructed the church members to offer to the others around them, "If I walked down there with you, would you be ready and willing to go down and publicly commit your life to Jesus right now?" We then started singing again and about three dozen people moved into the aisles and toward the front of the room. In the middle of that sea of faces was the woman, fresh out of jail, who had stood by me in line waiting to get in. As the name of each person was called out, we cheered for them. During the next week, they would each receive a daily contact from the church, and about 90 percent of them would be back to begin a catechism of sorts the following Sunday.

I share that image of a great invitation because we have come to the end of the main body of this book. I have laid before you six clear choices. Now I wish to invite you to do something with what you have read. Something specific. Beyond the group study you yet may convene, beyond the ministry coach you yet may hire, I want you to choose to do something here and now, something specific and significant, something that will signify that you are ready to draw your line in the sand and to refuse to lead a dying church.

When the choices are difficult, sometimes we opt not to choose but to simply remain in perpetual indecision. I want to invite you to make a choice.

The six choices are, again:

- Choosing life over death
- Choosing community over isolation
- Choosing fun over drudgery

- Choosing bold over mild

- Choosing frontier over fortress

- Choosing now rather than later

You have probably already made at least one of these choices a clear and compelling part of your life and mission. Name that choice aloud, and celebrate the good fruit in your life that comes of that choice. Share this with a friend. Or, if you are reading this book in solitude, share it with God, and celebrate!

Now, name an additional choice that has captured your attention and imagination as you have considered these pages. What is it about that choice that is scary to you or holding you back? Why is it that you sense God's Spirit, perhaps, stirring deep in your soul around this issue? Who is the person with whom you could visit candidly about this choice, who could offer feedback and accountability to support your decision? I urge you to make this choice. Furthermore, I urge you not only to make this choice, but to make this choice public—to share with a peer, to share with trusted members of your church, to share with me (paulnixon@juno.com) or with somebody on this planet who cares—so that you will mark this moment as significant. Share the choice that you are making, the thing that distinguishes this day forward from all the days that have come before, the line you are drawing in the sand.

Here you stand, you can not do otherwise. You henceforth refuse to serve as an accomplice to any church's slow demise. You refuse to serve a dying church.

EPILOGUE

A Conversation with Three Judicatory Leaders

Within most mainline denominational communities, there are pockets of hope beyond the isolated experiences of thriving local churches here and there. In these final pages, I have invited three leaders from rare *thriving regions* within three different denominations to reflect on the ideas presented in this book in light of their experience. In addition to representing different denominations, they also come from three different corners of the United States. They are Dr. Paul Borden, executive director of American Baptist Churches of the West (a regional body serving northern California and northern Nevada, including the San Francisco Bay area, a judicatory recently renamed Growing Healthy Churches), Bishop Larry Goodpaster of Alabama–

West Florida Conference of the United Methodist Church (serving the southern half of Alabama and western end of Florida), and the Reverend Paul Nickerson, an associate conference minister of the Massachusetts Conference of the United Church of Christ (serving the state of Massachusetts, including, of course, the Boston metropolitan area).

In the conversation that follows, we see, first, what is occurring in these three denominational regions and, second, the way these three judicatory leaders think about and foster such thriving churches.

THE GOOD NEWS ABOUT THESE REGIONS

American Baptist Churches of the West/Growing Healthy Churches was a region in steady decline until 1997. A decade ago, thirty-seven out of two hundred churches here were growing. Today, there are 153 steadily growing churches. Thirty-five new congregations have been started. Worship attendance has increased from thirty thousand to forty-two thousand. The number of new members by profession of faith in Christ has increased from eight hundred annually to two thousand. Several congregations have grown from less than one hundred to more than five hundred in worship attendance. To my awareness, no other denominational region in American history has ever before experienced this kind of turnaround.

Alabama–West Florida Annual Conference of the United Methodist Church, happens to be the region where I work as a congregational developer. During a thirty-year period when the UMC nationally experienced decline of 18 percent, Alabama–West Florida posted net membership *gains* of 18 percent—admittedly modest gains for a thirty-year period, but steady nonetheless, year after year. The number of churches averaging 350 or more in attendance has increased by 150 percent since 1974. The four largest congregations account collectively for more than eleven thousand persons weekly in worship. (These four gathered only about five hundred worshipers thirty years ago.) To my awareness, no other region in United Methodism has experienced such steady growth in recent times. Notably, this region has not seen the explosive metropolitan population growth associated with major cities like Atlanta and Tampa.

Massachusetts Conference of the United Church of Christ has historically experienced membership and attendance decline that parallels the larger experience of the United Church of Christ. However, in the last few years, about one hundred of their four hundred churches are showing net growth. Five new congregations have been started. A sixth new church is in the works—the first new church in the Congregational heritage to be planted on Cape Cod in many decades. Net membership gains in Massachusetts have been offset by congregations choosing to leave the denomination. However, a spirit of hopefulness is spreading in the region.

THE CONVERSATION

PAUL NIXON: Thank you each for agreeing to share with us a bit of what is happening among the churches you serve. The experiences of your three regions differ. *Thriving* is a relative term—and undoubtedly each of us prays and works for still more vibrant congregations and more societal impact. However, each of your regional bodies is seeing new life in your churches that exceeds the norm within your respective denominational tribes and within your respective parts of the nation. Tell us what you are doing from the conference or convention level to help create a climate conducive to helping local churches thrive and to bucking the national trends in your denominations.

PAUL BORDEN: In ABC Churches of the West, we have done three things. First, we have created an environment where pastors who desire to lead growing churches are constantly given the resources they need. The resources are training, training, and more training. Second, we take the arrows directed at those making this choice. Our pastors know they are not alone. Third, we have set up strong accountability systems for pastors. Pastors that are effective are honored and supported. We have made our pastors of our larger effective congregations our heroes. They mentor our small church pastors (which leads back to number 1, training).

PAUL NICKERSON: Taking arrows is important. For new life to happen in our churches, we in the middle judicatory have to be the best cheerleaders of those pastors and leaders who are willing to risk much for Jesus. If I am to be effective as a coach, a church needs to know that I am firmly standing with them, cheering them on to go deeper and go out into the mission field. Often in UCC circles there is more energy around "issues" than there is good coaching for church vitality. My only agenda as a conference leader is for the faithful development of congregations who are willing to live out the vision God has given them.

LARRY GOODPASTER: Resolutions, petitions, and legislative action will not change the current direction. Relationships, grace, and loving responses to the emotional, spiritual, and physical needs of people will bring life.

NIXON: Perhaps our most effective leverage as leaders is not contained in the official declarations in our denominational meetings, but in the way we live out our values in the context of thriving congregations in local communities.

NICKERSON: Yes, all the denominational hoopla isn't worth much in comparison to having a deep and caring heart for vital congregations.

GOODPASTER: In the Alabama–West Florida Conference of the UMC, one of our intentional decisions has been to encourage longer tenures for our pastors in one place. The average length of pastoral appointment (to one place) in this conference is more than double the national average for United Methodists, with an average of nine years in our largest churches. Some of our largest churches are served by pastors who were appointed to those churches fifteen to thirty years ago. A second intentional decision has been to start new churches. We have failed in some cases. We have succeeded more often than not. A third intentional effort has been to highlight, celebrate, encourage, and provoke membership growth and professions of faith. The process used to appoint a pastor in our conference takes into account the results of evangelism and outreach ministries where she or he is currently assigned.

NICKERSON: In the Massachusetts Conference of the UCC, there has been a focus on turnaround congregations and new church starts for fourteen years, as evidenced by a conference staff position focused on these concerns, in the context of a creative and innovative conference staff. The conference has invested time and money in the training of twenty Vitality Coaches who work with our congregations, plus bringing in top-flight trainers and ministry practitioners to train our leaders. I do want to say right at the start that I don't feel that the Massachusetts Conference has done the kind of turnaround Paul Borden has done. We are still "turning the ship."

NIXON: I hear two of you underlining your region's intentionality about resourcing local churches and pastors for effectiveness. Larry, you also have done this when you created my position as director of congregational development in Alabama–West Florida. True?

GOODPASTER: Yes, I vividly recall the conversation you and I had over coffee at a now-closed franchised restaurant. We were inviting you to leave the appointment that had brought you from Texas to Florida (and where you had served for nine years), and lead a new office in our conference structure focused on congregational development. Our conference had adopted a vision: "to cultivate dynamic, thriving congregations." I was keenly aware of the need for a creative, highly effective leader to guide this conference-wide priority. One-third of your time is focused on helping us plant new churches and faith communities. Two-thirds of your time is devoted to coaching and consulting with pastors and churches as they move toward health and vitality. The results of this ministry are everywhere evident across our area.

NIXON: Beyond coaching and training leaders, you each mention starting new churches. The rate of new church starts has increased in each of your regions under your leadership. "Choosing life over death" involves choosing to reproduce, choosing to birth new congregations into the existing community of congregations. Without the new church factor, I feel safe in saying that none of your areas would have stood out from the pack over the last few years.

GOODPASTER: Every time a church says "I think we are just about the right size," it has chosen death over life. Every time a church believes "we might get so big that we will not know everyone" it has opted for decline and death. Every time a church says "we may attract the wrong kind of people" it has chosen death over life. Every time a church says, "Don't start another church near us who might take some of our members," it is choosing death.

NIXON: Choosing life over death is one of the six choices we have explored in this book. Which of these six choices have you found important in your work?

BORDEN: The three that resonate most with me are choosing life over death, choosing bold over mild, and choosing now rather than later. In terms of the first, choosing life over death, we work only with congregations that desire to live, to be transformed, and to reproduce. We have gotten rid of all other things that get in the way of this mission. We do not waste time on churches that refuse transformation. We have also sold our camps and reduced our bureaucracy.

NIXON: Wow! When your region sells its camps, you send a signal that you are getting serious. Your focus is in the local parish and not in church life behind the front lines of ministry. That's a bold move.

BORDEN: In terms of boldness, every church or denominational entity faces pain. The question is, do we want our pain slowly over time or do we want to get it all at once? We have learned that Jesus was right. If you boldly choose to get it all at once and are willing to die for him you then find life. We have had our share of pain. But as a result we—meaning our pastors, our congregations, and our region—are living life to the fullest.

GOODPASTER: Not everyone has been in agreement with some of the statements and actions that I have had to make over the course of the last six years. I am convinced that this time in which we live and move and serve, this culture in which we operate, and the challenges facing believers today require—demand—bold action. Some will not like it at all. Some will wait it out, knowing that eventually this bishop will leave. There will be some who understand that it is all about the vision; it is all about Jesus; it is all about responding to human need by following Jesus; it is all about a calling, not a career. The status quo not only means more of the same, it means accelerating down the road to decline and death.

BORDEN: Old, dead, sick, dysfunctional congregations are like old drunks. You never get their attention if you are not bold.

NIXON: That was pretty bold, Paul—and it certainly got my attention!

BORDEN: The state of most congregations and denominations today causes the reputation of our God to be tarnished, not enhanced. If we say we have "good news," then we need to live that way. If we do not choose to trust God and make those choices that bring life, health, and growth, then it is better to walk away and stop doing that which ruins the name of our God. I believe we do not have the choice to maintain the status quo.

NICKERSON: Choosing bold over mild has also been important in my work. So many New England congregations have been in existence for 300 or 350 years. There is still a mentality that all we have to do is sit here in our churches and people will somehow just show up.

NIXON: We often say that some of our churches are living in the 1950s—I guess it is quite possible in an area where congregations have such long histories, to live *in the 1850s* mentally, and even liturgically. But we can't assume that anyone is going to wander through our doors or pay any attention to our pronouncements, like they might have done back in the Christendom era.

NICKERSON: This is why so much of my work has been to shake that tree. I must constantly teach a message of transformation and doing church in a new way. I have gotten in trouble with superiors and colleagues for pushing evangelism, for encouraging churches to take chances, and for mentioning Jesus so much. But there is no greater experience than to be working with a church or a cluster of churches and seeing the "light" come on when talking about a core discipleship process or how to get out into the community.

NIXON: Do you find the choice for boldness to be scary?

NICKERSON: Yes, sometimes. There is way too much fear in ministry—fear of not being liked, fear of losing one's job, fear of losing prestige, fear of losing a pension. As one of my mentors, Tom Bandy, has often said, we need to be ready to risk the parsonage and the pension for the wild and woolly ride of walking with Jesus into the mission field. There is no greater calling than taking this ride.

BORDEN: And no greater urgency! The third choice that is important for me is choosing now over later. I am getting near retirement age. I do not have time to wait. I will meet Jesus sooner than later. Therefore I'd better work for now because there is no later.

Nixon: Each of you is in your mid-fifties or beyond. This is common for judicatory leaders. You get a rather narrow window in time to try to make a difference.

Borden: By the way, the three choices that I have mentioned make ministry and life fun. I disagree with the notion that fun is a choice, at least for me. For me, fun is a result of other good choices.

Nixon: I will think about that. There is much yet to discover and to reconsider in conversation with others. Along those lines, *are there other key choices that any of you would add to the six I have outlined here?*

Nickerson: I would urge pastors, especially, to choose to pray and discern, to seek and follow the Spirit's leadership.

Nixon: We might call that "Choosing Holy Spirit over Personal Ego," the choice of spiritual listening. You all in the UCC are the folks who remind us of the fact that *God Is Still Speaking* in your public relations materials. It is amazing how easy it is for us pastors to stop listening to God once we discover an approach to ministry that works well in a particular place and time—only to find that times and places change.

Goodpaster: A seventh choice that I would add is choosing creativity and flexibility over same-old-same-old.

Nixon: That also sounds like a Holy Spirit thing.

GOODPASTER: Yes it is. This choice opens the door to new, fresh movements of God's Spirit. It celebrates the fact that God is constantly doing new things among the faithful ones. This choice arises from the awareness that it is not only insane to expect different results from doing the same thing; it is fatal.

The churches that are dynamic and thriving across our area—the very churches whose growth in members, mission, and ministry more than offset the declining churches in this conference—understand and practice creative ways of sharing and living the gospel of Jesus Christ. We have given permission to our people to put together a plan that works for them, provided it is within the broad scope of who we are as a church and as part of the connection of Methodism. We pray for one another; we support one another; but we have thrown out the cookie cutters.

NIXON: Paul Borden, do you see any additional key choices that are critical for those of us who lead twenty-first-century churches?

BORDEN: I think if I would add one I would say something about vision. By this I mean I would choose to dream rather than just living with the present. Vision is God's way of providing hope. Without hope it is often hard to be motivated. Therefore, I have chosen to dream and then let God lead to see if the dream will become reality.

NIXON: I find it interesting that you point to the necessity of *choosing* to dream. Sometimes we assume, too quickly, that dreams choose us. It certainly works both ways. "Choosing to Dream of God's Preferred Future rather than to Settle for the Present": That would have been a long chapter title, but I agree with you that this is a critical choice—and I considered developing a chapter around the need for visioning and vision-casting. In fact, if this conversation had not come so late in the publishing process, I might be tempted to add this as a seventh key choice.[17]

Again, thank you each for reflecting on the critical choices necessary to lead thriving movements as denominational officers.

17. I explore both these themes of listening to God and dreaming with God in my next book, *Mother Tongue,* which I hope will soon be published.

Additional Leadership Resources from
The Pilgrim Press

ALLIGATORS IN THE SWAMP
Power, Ministry, and Leadership

GEORGE B. THOMPSON, JR., EDITOR
Foreword by Andrew Young
Explores the issue of power and how it challenges ministry.
ISBN 0-8298-1671-2/Paper/208 pages/$21.00

HOW TO GET ALONG WITH YOUR CHURCH
Creating Cultural Capital for Doing Ministry

GEORGE B. THOMPSON, JR.
Ways in which pastors can invest themselves deeply into how their church does its work and ministries.
ISBN 0-8298-1437-X/Paper/176 pages/$17.00

A SPIRITUAL COMPANION TO
HOW TO GET ALONG WITH YOUR CHURCH

BEVERLY THOMPSON
Foreword by George B. Thompson, Jr.
A spiritual guide to strengthen the usefulness and effectiveness of the bestselling church leadership resource *How to Get Along with Your Church: Creating Cultural Capital for Doing Ministry*
ISBN 978-0-8298-1711-9/Paper/144 pages/$17.00

HOW TO GET ALONG WITH YOUR PASTOR
Creating Partnership for Doing Ministry

GEORGE B. THOMPSON, JR.

Practical ways to deal with conflicts that arise between pastor and congregation.

ISBN 978-0-8298-1713-3/Paper/144 pages/$17.00

TREASURES IN CLAY JARS
New Ways to Understand Your Church

GEORGE B. THOMPSON, JR.

Foreword by James Fowler

A paradigm-shifting resource for those in training in local church ministry.

ISBN 0-8298-1566-X/Paper/224 pages/$21.00

CAN THIS CHURCH LIVE?
A Congregation, Its Neighborhood, and Social Transformation

DONALD H. MATTHEWS

The story of a church that struggled to survive within a changing community.

ISBN 0-8298-1648-8/Paper/112 pages/$14.00

CHALLENGING THE CHURCH MONSTER
From Conflict to Community

DOUGLAS J. BIXBY

Discusses the ways in which churches can restructure themselves and work through conflicts that detract from the mission and vision of the church.

ISBN 0-8298-1506-6/Paper/128 pages/$16.00

HOPE IN CONFLICT
Discovering Wisdom in Congregational Turmoil

DAVID R. SAWYER

Valuable church leadership tool that helps leaders identify and lead with hope in conflict.

ISBN 0-8298-1758-4/Paper/176 pages/$20.00

LEADERSHIP FOR VITAL CONGREGATIONS
Congregational Vitality

ANTHONY B. ROBINSON

This book, the first in a new series of resources to guide clergy and lay leaders in creating vital congregations, focuses on leadership styles, approaches, and strategies.

ISBN 978-0-8298-1712-6/Paper/128 pages/$12.00

SOLOMON'S SUCCESS
Four Essential Keys to Leadership

KENNETH L. SAMUEL

Shares Solomon's four keys of leadership found in 1 Kings: wisdom, work, worship, and witness.

ISBN 978-0-8298-1572-6/Paper/112 pages/$15.00

BECOMING A PASTOR
Forming Self and Soul for Ministry

JACO J. HAMMAN

Explores and defines the complicated work involved in actually becoming a pastor.

ISBN 978-0-8298-1749-2/Paper/192 pages/$22.00

WHEN STEEPLES CRY
Leading Congregations through Loss and Change

JACO J. HAMMAN

Proper mourning of loss and change in churches is a vital
and life-giving aspect of healthy church leadership.

ISBN 0-8298-1694-1/Paper/192 pages/$21.00

---

*To order these or any other books from
The Pilgrim Press, call or write to:*

THE PILGRIM PRESS
700 PROSPECT AVENUE
CLEVELAND, OH 44115-1100

PHONE ORDERS: 800-537-3394 (M–F, 8:30 AM–4:30 PM ET)
FAX ORDERS: 216-736-2206

Please include shipping charges of $5.50 for the first book
and 75¢ for each additional book.

Or order from our web site at www.thepilgrimpress.com

Prices subject to change without notice.